We Will Not Cease
THE NEW ZEALAND CLASSIC

We Will Not Cease

THE NEW ZEALAND CLASSIC

By Archibald Baxter

FOREWORD BY MICHAEL KING

Eddie Tern Press

This North American edition of *We Will Not Cease* would not have
been possible without the help of the following people: Geoff Walker,
publishing director at Penguin Books (NZ); Dr. Stuart D. Lee at
Oxford University; Philip Dutton of the Imperial War Museum;
Dr. Michael King for his preface and comments; Terence Baxter;
Candace O'Connor for her exceptional editing; Peter Hoar at Auckland
University of Technology for his observations and invaluable research
on the footnotes, and, finally and most of all, Christine Catley of Cape
Catley Publishing for her unflagging enthusiasm for this project.

COVER DESIGN AND BOOK LAYOUT: Elizabeth Watson
MAPS: Gray Mouse Graphics
COVER PHOTO: Lieutenant Ernest Brooks, courtesy of the Imperial
War Museum. "The Somme Offensive, 1916. Battle of Bazentine Ridge.
British and German wounded on their way to the Dressing Station;
near Bernafay Wood, 19th July 1916."

Contents

Preface 7
Foreword 12
Maps 16, 17

Chapter

1 19

2 35

3 67

4 78

5 93

6 115

7 141

8 167

9 177

10 188

11 209

Afterword 222
Bibliography 223

Preface

WHEN WORLD War One ignited in 1914 and set in motion the events described so powerfully in this book, Archibald Baxter was a 33-year-old farm laborer on the other side of the globe from the scene of conflagration. His father and his maternal grandparents, the McColls, had been part of a chain migration of Scots to the southern parts of New Zealand in the mid-nineteenth century. Gaelic-speaking Highlanders, they made new homes in the province of Otago, a focus of Scottish Free Church settlement from 1848.

Archie Baxter's immediate family was large (he had seven siblings) and poor. He was required to leave school at age twelve and follow his father into a variety of casual and seasonal farming occupations: thinning turnips, shearing sheep, shooting rabbits, plowing. What he did take from his education, however, and nurture for the rest of his life, was a love of poetry—of Burns, Shelley, Byron, Blake, and later Henry Lawson, whose works he would recite as he labored in the open air.

In the course of the South African War at the turn of the twentieth century, however, Archie chanced to hear a speech by a Dunedin lawyer and Member of Parliament, probably A.R. Barclay. This experience turned his life in a new direction: toward pacifism. So strongly did he come to feel about the issue, and so persuasively to argue it, that he convinced his clannish family to adopt the same position at a time when the community at large was caught up in a spirit of imperial jingoism.

By 1914 his conscientious objection to military service was based on both pacifist and Christian socialist arguments.

When the wartime coalition government in New Zealand compiled a national register in 1915, six of the seven Baxter brothers affirmed that they would not serve in the armed forces (the seventh was married and therefore not immediately eligible for service). The following year all six were arrested after being drafted into a program of military conscription; so well-known were Archie's views that he was taken into custody before he had received his call-up papers.

He argued his case for exemption from service on the grounds of the teachings of Christ ("Thou shalt not kill"; "Turn the other cheek"; "Do good to them that hate you"). However, because he was not a communicant member of a religious body that believed all armed service was contrary to divine revelation, his appeal was turned down. He was moved from prison to prison, and then to Trentham Military Camp. From there he was shipped overseas and, eventually, taken to the front line of battle in France in an effort to break his spirit. "It's your submission we want, Baxter, not your service," one officer told him. In France he was subjected to a variety of disciplinary measures including the barbaric "Field Punishment No. 1," known to the troops as "crucifixion," in which he was bound to an outdoor post for up to four hours a day, inclined forward so that the weight was painfully borne by his arms and shoulder muscles. He was also beaten, denied food and medication, and sent to a section of the front that was undergoing heavy bombardment.

In April 1918 Archie was dragged from the mud by two British soldiers and placed in a hospital in Boulogne. He displayed symptoms of what would now be recognized as a post-traumatic stress disorder. At the time he was judged to be suffering from "mental weakness and confusional insanity." This diagnosis may have saved his life by preventing a court-martial which could have ended in his execution. He was moved to a British hospital for mentally disabled soldiers;

and finally, in August 1918, he was put on a troopship for return to New Zealand.

This book, Archie Baxter's recollections of the period, closes with the words, "And so my experiences in the army ended." In fact, the effects of his wartime treatment remained with him for a considerably longer time. His future wife, Millicent Macmillan Brown, met him in 1920 and noted that he had grown a mustache to disguise his untreated and decaying teeth, and that his eyes "protruded like those of crayfish" as a result of the strain of his experiences. They married in 1921, she a university professor's daughter who had herself studied in Sydney and Cambridge, Archie still a largely self-educated farm laborer. Though the teeth were replaced and the eyes eventually resumed their normal appearance, Archie continued for many years to be awakened by bad dreams and episodes of night-time sweating. And, for more than a decade, husband and wife had to endure harassment from officialdom because of Archie's principled wartime stand.

With his savings from almost three decades of farm laboring, the Baxters bought a farm at Kuri Bush on the Otago coast and lived near or in Brighton, close to the mouth of the Taieri River, for most of the rest of Archie's life. They raised two sons: Terence, who became a conscientious objector himself and underwent imprisonment in the course of World War Two; and the future poet James Keir Baxter, named Keir for Keir Hardy, whom both his parents admired. That younger son wrote of his father:

> ... I have loved
> You more than my own good, because you stand
> For country pride and gentleness, engraved
> In forehead lines, veins swollen on the hand;
> Also, behind slow speech and quiet eye
> The rock of passionate integrity.

It was the quietness, combined with the "passionate integrity," that most struck others who knew Archie Baxter over the rest of his long life. He was intimately involved in the Brighton community. He chaired the school committee, stood unsuccessfully for local body election, was an active member of the Labour Party, and, with Millicent, founded and actively promoted several anti-war groups.

We Will Not Cease was dictated by Archie to Millicent in Salisbury in 1937, when the family lived in England for a year. It was published by Victor Gollancz in London in 1939, but few copies reached New Zealand and most of the stock was destroyed in the Gollancz warehouse in 1941 during the Blitz. The book was republished by Caxton Press in Christchurch in 1968 as a result of enthusiastic lobbying by Philip Smithells, professor of physical education at Otago University, who was also a Quaker.

Archie Baxter, still active in retirement, wrote a foreword to the Caxton edition. Noting the nature of the Vietnam War, in which New Zealand was at that time engaged at the request of the United States, he said: "War has at last become wholly indiscriminate. The military machine is turned against that communal life which is the seed-bed of future generations of mankind." Cape Catley reprinted *We Will Not Cease* in 1980 and 1983, and arranged for an edition by CND Books, London, in 1986. Penguin New Zealand brought out another edition in 1987. This present edition is a joint publication of Eddie Tern Press in North America and Cape Catley in New Zealand.

We Will Not Cease has become a classic of anti-war literature because of the understated and affecting eloquence of its prose; and because, miraculously it would seem, it is devoid of rancor. Although Archibald Baxter occasionally lost his temper and his control in the course of the events he describes, he retained no bitterness. He writes of brutality more in sadness than in anger; and he is always at pains to point to the compassion with which he was treated by fellow prisoners and individual soldiers with whom he came into contact. His determination neither to cease nor to rest while the Christian ideal of peace remained unrealized, reflected in the words of Blake used for the book's title, was matched by a determination to forgive those who, in Archie's charitable view, knew not what they did. One of his major criticisms of the military machine was its potential to corrupt those caught up in its operations. It is this conjunction of activism and humanity, of force and grace, combined with a poet's preference for simplicity of language, that makes this book a great one.

Archibald Baxter died in 1970, having, with Millicent, followed his poet son into the Catholic Church a few years earlier. When Millicent turned ninety in 1978, somebody asked her what she would do if she were sixty years younger. Without hesitation she said, "I'd marry my husband again ... Archie has been the core of my life." She lived on to 1984, when she died at the age of ninety-six. James K. Baxter had predeceased her in 1972. At the time this edition went to press, only Terence survived from that family of four Baxters who spent a large portion of their lives together on the Otago coast. But the "seed-bed of future generations," of which Archie had spoken, was lustily and joyfully apparent in the florescence of grandchildren, great-grandchildren, and great-great-grandchildren who follow him and honor him.

—Dr. Michael King

Foreword

WHEN this book was first published, at the beginning of the Second World War, I sent a copy to Mark Briggs, who had suffered with me in France, with this inscription: "In memory of days that we can't yet afford to forget." Now that the book is being republished, the people who want this to be done will have various reasons for thinking it should be given again to the public. Some may consider its documentary value. Some may consider its literary value. In my own view the chief reason is still contained in the message that I sent to Briggs.

Throughout this half century the methods of warfare have steadily become more atrocious. Before the First World War people said to one another: "Warfare belongs to the past. Armies will never meet again with frontal attack in battle. We have too much respect now for human life." But in fact it has happened otherwise. A greater barbarism than any the human race had known in the past has risen among the nations. In the First World War multitudes of conscript* soldiers were buried alive in the mud of France. Villages were also annihilated. But the greatest number of casualties were among the conscript troops. In the Second World War the wholesale slaughter of civilians—by high explosives, by fire bombing, and finally by atomic weapons—became a matter of course. Reports from the present Vietnam War indicate that 80 percent of the casualties are occurring among civilians. War has at last become wholly indiscriminate. The military machine is turned against that communal life which is the seedbed of future generations of mankind. The only apparent

*Draftees.

justification that war ever had was that by destroying some lives it might clumsily preserve others. But now even that apparent justification is being stripped away. We make war chiefly on civilians and respect for human life seems to have become a thing of the past.

To accept this situation would be to accept the devil's philosophy. And, in fact, men are not accepting it easily. This book contains the record of my own fight to the utmost against the power of the military machine during the First World War. At that time to be a pacifist was to be in a distinct minority. But today—as war, which was always atrocious, becomes more obviously atrocious and anti-human—to be a pacifist is to be the spokesman even of a confused majority who have begun to see that, whatever the national issues may be, all wars are deeply atrocious and no war can be called just. Though methods of warfare have changed, the military machine remains essentially the same; and the record of my own battle against that machine, on behalf of my fellow-humans, is therefore relevant to this time also.

To oppose the military machine means to accept the possibility that one may be physically destroyed by it. In my own experience, the moment I recognized this clearly was when the military police showed me Briggs, with the enormous wound on his back, and said: "That's the way you'll be tomorrow." I did not think that Briggs would survive their deliberate violence, nor that I would survive it either. And I was able to accept this with a calm mind. I slept and woke again. Once I had accepted that ultimate fact, the military machine had no power at all over me. In fact, the blow did not fall as it had on Briggs, but came more slowly in another way: by starvation. But I had already made my decision at the time when I saw Briggs.

I remember always the gentleness and humanity of the ordinary soldiers who were close to me in those times. Once, when I had been maltreated by an officer while I lay on the ground, too weak to do otherwise, they carried me very gently, and quietly cursed the authorities who were punishing me. Later they were penalized for being too lenient with me. When three of them pulled me out of a shell hole and said: "Stick with us," I felt that I could not let them risk their own lives for me under a false impression, so I told them I was an objector. They said they knew all about me and understood quite well what I was standing for. The ordinary soldiers were not antagonistic. When I starved at the last, they too were near starving, but would certainly have given me some of their meager rations if I had told them of my situation. If the soldiers had not looked after me, I would undoubtedly have died. My feeling towards them resembles a prayer that something good might always follow them, and that the light should shine upon them. Nor, for that matter, do I have any feeling of hostility towards the officers whose duty it was to do me harm. They, unlike the soldiers, had become part of the military machine, had submerged themselves in it; and it was the military machine I was opposing, not them as persons.

There were two strange dreams, not mentioned in the book, which I had shortly before the outbreak of the First World War. In the first dream I was traveling on the road near my birthplace, when I heard a noise in the sky, and when I looked up I saw a huge human eye moving over the land, followed by a trail of black funeral crepe. The feeling associated with the dream was one of grief and horror. In the second dream I was again in the same place, and saw a vast forest of trees, straight and slim and tall, growing towards the sky. "They are more beautiful than any I have ever seen," I thought.

Then a man who stood by me answered my thought. "Yes, they are beautiful," he said, "but I am full of grief when I look at them. Those are the young men of the world, but the lords of the forest have sold it to death."

Dreams do not prove anything; but I remember that when the troopship, the *Waitemata* sailed out of Wellington Harbor, the noise of the propeller and the pounding of the sea was exactly the same noise that I had heard in the first dream. The dreams were perhaps premonitory; as if the grief that was to come through war to the people of this country had already touched my mind. The people have never truly welcomed war. If my own experience of that grief has helped in any way towards the abolition of war, it will not have been for nothing.

—*Archibald Baxter 1968*

Tasman Sea

Auckland●

NEW
ZEALAND

NORTH
ISLAND

UpperHutt
(Trentham prison)

◎Wellington
(Mount Cook prison,
Terrace prison)

Wellington Heads

●Christchurch

SOUTH

ISLAND

*Pacific
Ocean*

●Waikouaiti

Taieri River

●Otago
●Dunedin
Brighton
●Kuri Bush

N

MANY WEEKS BEFORE the war of 1914-18, I had reached the point of view that war—all war—was wrong, futile, and destructive alike to victor and vanquished. My first step on that path was taken in my early manhood, when I happened to listen to an address on and against war by a Dunedin lawyer, a brave and upright man, whose voice was as of one crying in the wilderness, so unlikely did it seem that his point of view would ever be accepted by more than the very few. However, the newspapers thought it worthwhile to attack him, and as proof that anti-militarist views were not, even then, altogether unpopular with the common people, he was returned to Parliament at the next election with a greatly increased majority.

For many a day I was without a single supporter, either in my pacifism or in the socialism which I looked on as a necessary part of it. There was no Labour Party. Only isolated radicals in and out of Parliament upheld what would now be the Labour point of view. We were geographically so far removed from Britain that we only had meager accounts of the rise of the Labour Party there. It was not until Keir Hardie came out to us in 1912 that the workers' party in Britain really meant very much to me.

I plowed a lonely furrow and for a long time did not even get the support of my own family. Gradually, however, they came to see there was something in what I said, all the more as they began to hear the same sort of thing from some of the members of the rising Labour Party.

I was, of course, outside the scope of the Act for the compulsory military training of boys and youths from fourteen upwards, which was introduced in New Zealand in 1911, but the strong and increasing opposition to it on the part of the boys themselves—in 1913 there were more than 7,000 prosecutions under the Act—encouraged me in thinking that there was an underlying objection to militarism amongst the people.*

In 1914 war came. My opposition to this war, and to all wars, was strengthened rather than diminished during the next two years, and I did not hesitate to give expression to it when I saw a chance of having any effect. I met in the most unexpected places people who were definitely opposed to the war, and people who had doubts, but fear usually prevented that opposition from being at all effective. If everyone who was definitely opposed to the war—all war and every war—would clearly and openly say so and stand to it, we should be a long way on the path of doing away with war.

In 1915 the National Register was taken. All men of military age were required to state whether they were willing to undertake military service. The men registered in this category numbered roughly 196,000. Of these, 33,700 said they would not undertake service at home or abroad, and 44,300 declared their willingness to undertake home service, but refused service abroad. I stated that I would undertake no service in the army, either at home or abroad, and in a brief note gave my reasons. The National Register was, of course, a

*At the start of the war the population of New Zealand was 1,147,000.

prelude to conscription, which was introduced the following year and brought into force at the close of 1916. I had seen it coming, as anyone who had thought at all must have seen it coming, for many a long day. It strengthened and focused my opposition. Men were now to be forced into the mass murder of war. The supreme denial of liberty was to be fastened upon us. I had long ago faced the knowledge that I would now be called upon actively to defend the principles I held.

It was impossible to foretell what would happen. I did not have the experience of the English objectors to guide me—not that it would have been a guide, as my experience, at least, was fated to be different—for very little about them reached us through the newspapers, and I was not in touch either with anti-militarist organizations or with the political Labour Party, both of which were able to obtain more information. I did not even know whether I would have any companions in my stand. I hoped my brothers would be with me, but until the time of testing comes, one can be certain of no one but oneself—and not always even of that.

As for exemption, I knew there was no hope for it. The Appeal Boards were farcical as far as objectors were concerned, their members usually ridiculing the objectors who were rash enough to appeal. Only those who "had belonged on the 4th day of August, 1914, and had since continuously belonged to a religious body, the tenets and doctrines of which declare the bearing of arms and the performance of any combatant service to be contrary to divine revelation" had any right to exemption, and even then the exemption was only to combatant service. I belonged to no organized Church and did not base my beliefs on the teaching of any sect. To me, Christianity is based on the commandment:

"Thou shalt love thy neighbor as thyself."

I do not profess to be able to live up to this ideal, but one can at least go so far along the road as to try to treat other people as one would wish to be treated by them, and war cuts this position at its very roots.

Even if it had been possible to obtain exemption I would never have gone before an Appeal Board to plead my case, for I did not consider that any Board had the right to be judge of a man's sincerity.

I began to work my farm with a view to having to leave it in the near future, and in the summer of 1916-17, I took as much shearing as I possibly could, in order to leave a large check behind me. The people I was shearing for all knew my views and intentions, and were, many of them, very sympathetic. They were, some of them said, troubled at the thought of what lay before me. One man said: "What I am afraid of is that they'll get you away in cells, where no one will know anything about it, and batter the life out of you."

The opposition to war was stronger now than it had been in the first years, but it was, unfortunately, no more openly expressed than before. People expressed themselves to me because they knew already what my views were. But each man's fear of what his neighbor might think prevented any organized opposition, apart from a certain amount of political protest put up by the Labour Party. They opposed the passing of the Act, and opposed it even after it was put in force, and in consequence several of the leaders were serving sentences in prison for sedition.

Shearing over, I returned home towards the end of February. Under the sub-clause in the Conscription Act, popularly known as the Family Shirkers Clause, men belonging to families, no member of which had gone to the war, could be called up without first having appeared in the ballot, and I knew, of course, that this applied to us, and that any one of us was liable to get a calling-up notice at any time.* As far as I could ascertain, judging by the experience of others, I would have three weeks' respite after the arrival of the notice before I would be arrested, and that three weeks I intended to put in getting all my affairs in order. The longer I delayed in selling my lambs and my crops the better price I would get for them, and the more money I would be able to leave behind me. That arranged for, I should be ready for whatever lay before me.

A few days after my return, I was coming over the rise behind the house, carrying my rifle, which I had been using to frighten the birds from the crop. Just below me appeared the local policeman, holding a paper in his hands above his head. "It's all right, Archie, it's all right," he called. "I just want to see you about these statistics."

I filled in the paper for him, puzzled at his obvious agitation and alarm, the reason for which appeared later. The following morning I was getting ready to go into the sale yards. My horse was feeding in the yard outside, and I was in my shirt sleeves, washing my face, when the policeman appeared at the door. "Just something more to do with these statistics, Archie! Come down here out of the wind."

As we came near the hedge, another policeman sprang out from behind it and they seized me. "You're under arrest!"

"All right. Let me go and get my things."

"No fear, you're not going back to the house, you're coming with us."

"Well, one of you go to the door and ask for them."

But they refused and pulled me down to the road where their cart was waiting. My father, who had come out, said to them: "What do you mean, telling me these lies?"

"You mind what you're about, or you'll be arrested too."

He fell silent, rather to my surprise, for he was the last man on earth to be silenced by threats. Long afterwards, he

---
*Baxter was 33 at the time.

told me that it was not fear for himself, but fear that they would take it out on me, if he said any more, that silenced him, and I could well understand it. My mother and sister came out with my coat and hat. There was no time for farewells. I took my place between the two policemen in the cart and we drove off. My mother came running down to the gate with something in her hand. After one glance, the two men bent double in the cart and whipped up the horse to a gallop. I looked round and laughed; they were so ridiculous in their terror. "Don't be frightened. It's only a book she wants to give me."

After they had gone some distance, one of them looked round and said: "It's all right, stop," and they pulled up. "We thought it was a revolver."

I did not know then, and I do not know now, where the idea of violent resistance on our part, and particularly on my part, originated. The idea was persistent. Four months later, when two of my brothers were arrested—they were away working at the time of my arrest—two carloads containing twelve policemen, military and civil, were thought necessary for the carrying out of the operation. As they crept nervously up the garden in the darkness, the local policeman fell into one of the enormously deep trenches my father always made when he dug the garden, and was, poor man, convinced, I am sure, that this was a specially set trap and only the beginning of the general massacre of all of them. His state of excitement and agitation when he arrived at the house, covered in clay, was a proof of this. All this, I only heard long afterwards.

As we drove along, the two men tried to excuse their panic. "We heard you were going to resist arrest," they said.

"If I had been meaning to resist, you wouldn't have got me so easily. I could have cleared out months ago if I'd wanted to. You've treated me very unfairly, arresting me like this. I counted on three weeks' warning."

They laughed at the idea of giving me warning. They had been hearing about me, they said, for months past, and had been told that I had said openly that I was going to defy the military and would never serve in the army. I asked them if they thought it was likely that I would have talked so openly if I had been meaning to slip away and get out of it. We argued all the way in. The local policeman, who, I afterwards heard, was a Theosophist, assured me that taking part in war would not jeopardize my chances in the next life.

We drove to the Kensington Drill Hall in Dunedin, a distance of about twelve miles, and I was handed over to the military authorities. A guard of four men with bayonets fixed took me to the St. Kilda Battery. We marched down the middle of the principal street, arousing plenty of interest and comment in the passers-by. The future held many worse experiences in store for me, worse from every point of view, but nothing ever cut me again like that first, deliberately indicted, public humiliation. We reached the Battery and I was shut in a cell. They brought me something to eat, but I couldn't touch it, though I was very thirsty and thankfully drank the tea. That first night has remained a bitter memory. The first adjustment to entirely different conditions is always hard, and these were so utterly different from those of the normal life I had left behind me that morning. No amount of preparing oneself beforehand can remove the sting of the first realization that freedom is lost, that one's body has passed from one's control, that others possess it and can do their will with it; the consciousness of the locked door and all that it implies. Gradually one becomes hardened and a protective tissue grows over one's first extreme sensitiveness. At the same time a price has to be paid for that hardening process.

Late that evening my brother Jack arrived at the Battery from Central Otago. The rumors of the violence with which we were supposed to be going to resist arrest had evidently not reached there. Jack had been arrested by a single apologetic policeman, whose only desire had been to make himself and his prisoner as little conspicuous as possible. The old Irish sergeant in charge at the Battery had said to him when he came in: "There's a man here I'm sorry for: he's taking it very hard."

The next day we were taken by lorry to the station, pausing at the Drill Hall to collect two returned soldiers who were being sent into camp under arrest.

As the train ran down beside the harbor I looked out at the familiar landmarks and wondered if I would ever see them again. The motion had a soothing effect. My mind relaxed from its tension and I watched the landscape passing the window as though in a dream. Not that we were without incident to enliven the journey. At Waikouaiti a man in dungarees with a badly crushed ankle was delivered over to our escort who, rightly or wrongly, regarded the injury as deliberate and laughed at his angry complaints.

"What do they mean," he cried, "sending a man to camp with a foot like this?"

"Don't you worry," they said. "Plenty of doctors in camp. They'll soon fix your foot for you, and you'll be as right as you were before."

The sergeant in charge of the escort proffered me well-meant consolation. "I've been making calculations," he said, "about the proportion of men killed in the war. It's not very high, not nearly as high as you'd think—no higher, in fact, than in lots of ordinary occupations. You only run one chance in five hundred of being killed. Now that's not much, is it?"

The military police, who had not been to the war themselves, were plainly in awe of their returned soldier charges, and allowed them to do pretty much as they liked, even to the extent of obtaining drink on the journey; with the result that one of them, already a little drunk, became much more so in the course of the day. He turned to me: "You waited 'til you were arrested, did you?"

"Yes."

"Well, you haven't got much time left. I can tell you exactly what will happen in your case; as soon as you get up there, you'll be shot."

"Is that so?" I said. "I wouldn't have thought they'd go as far as that. I hope there'll be a good report in the papers."

He was annoyed at being taken lightly.

"I tell you, you'll find what I say is right: You'll be shot."

He then held forth against the war, the military, and the police, with a strange reckless excitement, by no means entirely due to drink. He and his quieter mate both bore unmistakable signs of unnatural strain in their faces.

In those days, instead of dashing out at stations and bolting a hasty meal with an eye on the clock, to be summoned back to the train by the ringing of the bell, as we do now, one ate one's meal in comfort and leisure in the dining car, watching the scenery glide by outside. That pre-war luxury, along with many another, is now only a distant memory. The dinner in the dining car that day, I can remember very well, even to the vegetable marrow, which I found delicious, this being the first food I had been able to touch since I had left home.

We spent the night on the deck of the ferry and arrived at Trentham the following morning, being at once put in the guardroom. Shortly afterwards, I was brought before the Camp Commandant, charged with being absent without leave. I explained I had been arrested without any previous calling-up notice and had not had the time I had counted on to set my affairs in order. "Let me go down for three weeks," I said, "and I give you my word that I'll come back up here at the end of that time."

"And when you come back, will you agree to take on service in the army?" he asked.

I said, no, that I couldn't do that. In that case, he told me, nothing could be done about it, but as I should have had a calling-up notice the charge against me would be wiped out.

The guardroom housed a heterogeneous collection. Drunks, fierce men loudly denouncing the war and the army, but ready in the end to take it on, and others, equally fierce, who said we ought to be shot. We were almost the first of the men who had thought the matter out and definitely made up their minds to resist military service; but before we had been there long, they were beginning to come in. In a few days time my youngest brother Sandy was brought into camp. Warned by my fate and determined not to be taken unawares, he had kept a sharp lookout, had noticed the arrival of two policemen and, by the time he saw them crawling up the garden on their hands and knees, had almost finished his preparations for the journey. The three of us, together with Little, a young fellow from the far north, who for some reason was always included in our company, were taken down to the Stores and offered our kits.* We all refused them and were taken back to the guardroom. Up until then we had had the freedom of the guardroom and the yard, could walk about and sit down where we pleased. Now, however, we were each ordered into a cell and the door locked.

A bucket of water had just been thrown into my cell, with the object of making it unpleasant for me, and the floor was soaking. There was nothing whatever to sit down on and, as I could not sit on the wet floor, I had to spend my whole time pacing up and down in the small space or leaning against the wall.

---

* "Taking up the kit" and "putting on the uniform" are the same. If he accepts this, the military has won a victory and he is that much closer to obeying orders—the real defeat as the point of his stand is to bring into question the authority of those commanding.

We were again offered our kits and again refused them and were returned, as before, to our cells. This time I asked for my overcoat, which was hanging up in the guardroom, and used it to sit down on.

We were now brought before the Colonel, formally charged with disobeying an order. I explained that my refusal was part of my general refusal to take on any service whatever in the army. The other three said their attitude was the same as mine.

"If you were in Germany, you'd be shot," said the Colonel. "Twenty-eight days detention."

We were taken down to Wellington and marched through the streets to the Alexandra Barracks. On arrival we were ordered by the Corporal in charge to change into denims.

"What do we want denims for?" I asked. "Our own clothes are good enough."

"You want them to work in."

"But I don't intend to do any work under military orders."

The others said the same. We were taken before the Major in command, charged with disobeying an order, and sentenced to three days bread and water and to be deprived of our mattresses. We were then locked in our cells which were in the top story of the high building. The windows were large and admitted plenty of light and air and we could get a good view of the town through them. There were no bars, escape not being considered possible from that height.

There we spent the next three days, seeing no one but the guard who brought us bread and water. At night, not being allowed mattresses, we slept on the floor in our blankets. I did not eat the bread, as I refused to submit to the humiliation of this sort of punishment. This was not noticed until the evening of the third day, when the guard, bringing me in my final bread ration, saw the pile of it in the corner. "Where on earth did you get all this bread?"

"It's what you've brought me every day."

"And you haven't eaten any of it?"

"No, and I don't intend to. It's not the sort of fare I am accustomed to."

That night I was given a cup of tea and a chop. The next day, our sentences being up, we were allowed out on the landing. I asked the others if they had had any chops. They had not, and they had eaten the bread. If they had known I was hunger-striking, they would have struck, too.

Though we now mixed with the other prisoners on exercise and at meals, which we ate in common, we were still locked up while they were at work. The N.C.O. in charge argued with me on the subject of obeying military orders. "If the military authorities chose to," he said, "they could compel you to obey."

"If I thought so, I would put myself out of their power."

I don't know what I meant by it. It was said on the spur of the moment to hold my end up in argument, and I had no intention of committing suicide. It was, however, taken as a threat of suicide. I was removed to a cell without a window, and when, a day or two afterwards, I was returned to my former one, I found that heavy iron bars had been cemented into the brickwork at the sides of the window. For some reason I was evidently suspected of meditating violence, for one of the guards when he unlocked my cell door, used to throw it open and spring back into the passage as if he expected me to be standing just inside ready to knock him down.

One attempt at escape was made from a cell in the same story while I was serving my sentence in the civil prison. The Irish objector who attempted the escape told me about it when I was back in the Barracks for the second time and he was back from the hospital. He was warm-hearted and full of kindly impulses. He once pushed a cold potato through the spyhole in my door when I was on bread and water. He told me that the effect on him of being shut up in a small place was to drive him to the verge of frenzy. It was madness, he knew, to attempt to jump from that height, but he was desperate. He made a rope of his blankets and tied it to a broom handle fixed against the window. When he was six feet below the window the knots gave way. By good luck he fell on to the telegraph lines, at that part fortunately not taut, rebounded from them, and fell on the pavement. If that had not happened he could not have escaped being killed. As it was, it was four days before he recovered consciousness.

We were allowed to have books brought in by visitors from outside. A guard came into my cell and found me reading Carlyle's *French Revolution*, which had come in this way. "Revolution!" he said. "You're not allowed that kind of book here," and seized it.

"Take it to the Major and ask him if I can have it." He went off with it, confident of victory. The book was returned soon afterward, without comment.

For meals we were locked in the mess room without a guard, and the food was distributed by two prisoners acting as orderlies. These two were religious objectors, for some reason not segregated like most of their religious comrades, but fallen amongst the goats, and as goats in the Biblical sense they certainly regarded us. I don't say they were typical of the narrowly religious objectors; I don't think they were. I daresay I was intolerant, but they irritated me by an attitude of smugness and complacency.

To return to the mess room—orders had been given at tea time that the Baxters were to have no rice or currants. The two orderlies kept back the amount that should have been given to us and ate it themselves. They always obeyed orders so implicitly that it was a puzzle to me how they ever came to be in detention barracks.

Newcomers were arriving all the time, bringing word

from Trentham* of the increasing number of objectors there. I heard much of one, Briggs by name, whom the authorities had sent straight to the civil prison with a month's sentence. No preliminary twenty-eight days detention. It was possible to pick him out quite easily from the yard of the Barracks, working at the Mt. Cook prison nearby. Would we go there next? That was one of the principal subjects of discussion amongst the prisoners. The idea of jail was rather a bugbear to some, and mothers were alarmed at the thought of their young sons doing prison sentences. But whatever we thought of it, it seemed very likely that that would be the next step.

To us it came sooner than to the others owing to our refusal to work in detention.

Before we had served half of our twenty-eight days, the Major, a quiet, delicate-looking man, came along to our cells and, obviously nervous and flustered, formally ordered me to scrub the corridor in front of the cells. I refused. So did the other three. We were taken before the doctor to be examined as to our fitness to undergo a court-martial sentence—a necessary formality according to military law.

He asked me: "Do you suffer from anything?"

"Not as a rule," I said. "I am pretty fit. Now and again I have a little rheumatism."

"Have you got it now?"

"Yes, a bit, in the hip. Probably the result of lying on the bare floor without a mattress."

"Yes, probably it is, and who is to blame for your not having a mattress but yourself? Fools you are, getting up against the authorities and refusing to serve your country. You deserve all you get."

I tried to put my side, but that only made him angrier. The next day we were brought down again before the doctor

---

*A major military camp in Upper Hutt. In the Great War it was where the infantry mustered and trained.

and the Commandant to have the charge read over to us. The doctor's report stated: "This man has complained of rheumatism. He has no acute rheumatism, and in my opinion, no rheumatism at all."

I was very angry and rushed in to the attack without realizing—in fact, at that time without knowing—what harm one can do oneself by antagonizing the one official who, above all others, holds the fate of the prisoner in the hollow of his hand.

"I did not complain," I cried. "I only mentioned it because you asked me. You know perfectly well you are not telling the truth in that report."

I knew very well I had made a bitter enemy, but I was only thinking of rectifying myself, and, in my ignorance, did not care.

Several days after this, we were marched down to the Buckle Street Barracks for court-martial. We were left for a time in the drill shed. There were several men about, and they started talking, obviously intending us to overhear.

"Well, I didn't think I'd ever have to make one of a firing party."

"No, it seems a pity, doesn't it, and two of them so young."

Here, knowing very well that this bluff was intended for us, I laughed, and, finding we were not taking them seriously, they joined in.

The members of the court were new to the job of trying objectors and doubtful of their ground. They gave me plenty of opportunity to state my case. I argued that, not having taken the oath, or agreed to take on service in the army, I was not a soldier and could not, therefore, be charged with disobeying the lawful command of a superior officer. I also pointed out that we had not finished our sentences at the Barracks, that the offense we had committed was an offense against the discipline of the Barracks, and that, legally, we should be punished according to the regulations in force there and not tried by an outside court. They held me up at intervals and held long discussions in whispers. Plainly they were nonplussed by my arguments. However, there was only one possible outcome, no matter what defense we put up. We were all found guilty and sentenced to eighty-four days hard labor in the civil prison.

2

THE TERRACE JAIL was a survival—and there are many such in the world—from the days when security, lack of light, and lack of air, seemed to be the main things aimed at in building a prison. High outer walls successfully cutting off sunlight and view from the yards. Then more walls, still further preventing the admission of light to the small, barred windows in the cells. The Terrace jail has now been pulled down, but as far as New Zealand is concerned, Mt. Eden jail in Auckland still remains, of very much the same type, and housing hundreds of men within its walls. Of country prisons in New Zealand I cannot speak, for I have had no experience of them.

We were marched in through the main gates to the reception office, where our escort formally delivered us over to the prison authorities. Several warders were present and one stern-looking individual in blue, the Chief Warder, an old army man.

"Are you men New Zealanders?" he asked us.

"We are," I answered.

"Then I wonder you're not ashamed to look a New Zealander in the face."

"I am not ashamed of looking anyone in the face," I was beginning, when he silenced me with a roar of "Shut your mouth! No back-chat from you!" and I had to submit. I had begun to realize that one need not expect to be treated as a human being here. Our particulars were taken. I said I did not belong to any organized Church and I did not notice at the time what they put down for me under the heading of religion. Next, an official seized me by the arm, and pulled me roughly over to a table. Holding my hand down, he pressed each finger with considerable force and weight, so that I felt as if the bones were being crushed, on to a sheet of some white substance. He did the same with the other hand and dusted the results with a black powder. Whereupon the fingerprints sprang clearly into view.

"By jove," I said, "that's pretty hot. They're actually taking our fingerprints!"

"Will you shut your mouth!" shouted the warder.

We were herded into an adjoining room where we were stripped to the skin. We were weighed and scrutinized for body marks, which were noted down where there were any. I believe that a prisoner on reception has usually to take a bath, but as we had come straight from another prison our cleanliness was presumably taken for granted. Our own clothes were taken away, every object in the pockets being carefully examined, noted, and put away, to be returned to us intact when we went out. We then put on the prison clothing: woolen underclothing, quite good of its kind; and outer garments, shapeless, ill-fitting, and badly patched in many places, consisting of a brownish coat and white trousers, plentifully bespattered with broad arrows.* The boots, too, were shapeless and hardly to be recognized as boots. We wore, whenever we were outside our cells, a white cloth cap just as shapeless

---

*Although stripes were used in the U.S., Britain and the Commonwealth countries tended to use uniforms with large arrowhead shapes on them.

as the clothes and the boots. The others, especially Jack, who put on an air of ferocity befitting the occasion, looked typical criminals. I could not see myself, perhaps fortunately, for I don't doubt I looked even worse. It is astonishing the difference that clothes and a haircut can make. A few minutes before, we had been ordinary citizens, unnoticeable in any particular. Now anyone would have picked us as belonging unmistakably to the criminal class.

We were marched along, clumping in our clumsy boots, through corridors and doorways, until we came to a hall in the main building, flanked by cells on either side. Here we were each locked in a cell. I had had some experience of cells in the preceding month, but this was infinitely worse than anything I had known. To begin with, the door was always shut with a resounding slam and locked with a great clashing of keys, producing a sense of the inexorableness of the grasp in which one was held. The cell itself, narrow, dark, and airless, gave me a feeling of physical oppression. The building was so large, the cell so small, that the walls seemed to be closing in upon one. The window—tiny, high up and closely barred—gave upon a wall; consequently, so little light found its way into the cell that it was hardly possible to read at midday. It contained a straw mattress, up-ended against the wall, and blankets folded neatly, a pillow, a stool, a shelf, a tin basin, and a tin chamber pot. I had not been long in the cell when the door was opened with more clashing of keys and dinner brought round by prisoner orderlies, escorted by a warder. It consisted of stew with vegetables and potatoes, quite wholesome. When we were taken out into the yard a little later, Jack whispered to me: "Well, the dinner wasn't too bad, anyway. Perhaps things won't be so bad here, after all."

The exercise yard was surrounded by high brick walls. On the roof was a pagoda-like structure, built to shelter the armed warder, who, from his position, could command the whole of the yard. For the first part of the exercise period the prisoners mingled together and talked indiscriminately amongst themselves; but on a given signal from the warder in charge, they formed into pairs and marched around and round the ring. At the side of the yard stood a row of W.C.s.* Anyone wishing to use them—and one was supposed to train oneself to do so at this time—shouted "Rear!" An interchange of shouts with the warder generally followed, depending on whether there was an unoccupied cubicle or not. In time we became quite accustomed to this public performance.

We were brought back and locked in our cells again. Soon afterwards, tea was brought round. It consisted, invariably, of a twelve-ounce loaf of new bread which had to last until the same time the following day, and a cup of nauseating bluish liquid without milk. It was bitter stuff, but one got used to it in time to a certain extent, for it had the advantage of being hot. Nothing else. It required a considerable exercise of self-control not to demolish the whole of the very moderately sized loaf at one go and leave nothing for breakfast. I noticed that the knife with which we were provided was of soft tin. This and the prohibition of razors was supposed to prevent the possibility of suicide. One could be shaved by the prison barber; but the experience of being shaved in cold water with a blunt razor by a prisoner who didn't care how he did the job, was so unpleasant that I only went for a shave when I was compelled to. As was to be expected under the circumstances, the shave was not a clean one, the stubble showing as soon as one left the barber's hands.

The tea, so-called, though I got used to it later, I felt that first time I could not touch. So, my cell door having been left open, I ventured out into the hall to get some water from the tap. An angry warder caught me just as I was drinking the first mouthful. "What are you doing out here? Get back to your cell!"

*Latrines.

"I only came out for a drink of water. I don't like the tea."

"Drink what you're given; you'll get nothing else, you understand that you don't come out of your cell unless you're told to."

We were locked up for the night. One could read, if one had a book, which I at first had not, until lights were turned out at nine. Otherwise there was nothing to do but sit and think or pace up and down between the door and the end wall, three paces up, three down, until it was time to go to bed. Sometimes there was a click, and the spy-hole shutter, operated from the outside, would open. If all was in order, as it usually was, the shutter clicked back into place and the warder's slippered feet passed on. I have known him to look in upon me three or four times in one half-hour, sure that he would at last catch me in some breach of the regulations. One night, to create a little diversion in the wearing monotony of those long evening hours, when I heard my neighbor's shutter click, I placed myself up against the door where I was out of sight from the spy-hole.

"Where are you, Baxter?" shouted the warder and, hastily unlocking the door, he threw it open, appearing in the doorway in great agitation. He was plainly relieved at the sight of me. "What do you mean, standing where I can't see you? Don't you know you're not allowed to do that?"

"Is that another regulation?" I asked. "I thought at least I had the freedom of the cell."

"You'll get something you won't like," he said, and slammed the door.

Those regulations! As every prisoner had to obey them it seemed only reasonable that there should be a copy in every cell. Far from it. We were not even allowed to read the copy pasted up in the hall. I tried to, but was driven away every time by the warder in charge. "No loitering in the passages." Finally, but starting every time where I had left off the time before, I managed to commit most of the printed form to memory. I don't know why there should be this objection to the prisoners knowing the regulations. Possibly because the warders are afraid of being held too strictly to them themselves.

That first night, when I started to go to bed, I found I had struck one of the worst things in my prison experience. No sheets, no pillowcase; only blankets, hard and brittle with age and much baking, and foul-smelling beyond belief. The pillow was a greasy, filthy bit of ticking, filled with small hard pellets of what appeared to be metal of some sort. I never found out what they were. The blankets were too old and hard to have much warmth in them. They were baked to destroy germs and lice, but the knowledge that the dirt and the odor were hygienic did not help me much that first night. In time I seemed to get accustomed to them. Or perhaps it was that I never struck anything quite so bad as those first ones.

Often during the night—and during all the nights I passed in prison—the silence was broken by horrible, long-drawn howls, expressive of pent-up misery, bitterness, hate. The warders rushed about, trying to locate the culprit. But they seldom succeeded. Such sounds echoing and re-echoing as they did were exceedingly difficult to trace to their source.

In the morning I was roused early, washed in the basin provided, and emptied the dirty water into the chamber pot. Shortly after, the door was unlocked, and I had to empty my slops into the tin brought round by the orderlies. The door was locked again, to be opened not long afterwards for breakfast.

A cupful of thin, watery porridge without milk or sugar and often without salt, the unappetizing tea, and whatever one had been able to preserve of the bread from the night before. Breakfast and tea never varied. For dinner one might sometimes have rice instead of potatoes. The entire absence

of fat in the diet resulted, on my part, in an abnormal craving
for any kind of fat. At the same time the smell of the stuff that
was used for greasing the boots made me sick, though I have
known men to eat it. If the absence of fat in the diet had such
an effect on me, what must it have had on men with long sentences? In some cases, long-sentence men reached a stage
when the prison allowance was more than they could eat, and
I have seen bread lying uneaten in their cells after they had
gone out. This implies, not an excessive allowance of food,
but an unhealthy condition of body and mind. Most of the
men who had been any length of time in the prison had a yellowish pallor as if they had been reared under a tub. There
was no outdoor work in the Terrace. Breakfast over, a prisoner, brought in by the warder, gave me a demonstration of
the proper way to fold my blankets, in a sort of symmetrical
cascade, with the stripes running exactly in sequence. Then I
had to do it in the same way, with the warder standing over
me and shouting at me if I failed in any particular. Afterwards
he gave me cloths and polish and told me to polish the steel
of the stairway. I made what I considered a very fair job of it
and went back to him.

"I've finished it. Have I done it all right?"

"Go on with your work," he said.

"But I've finished all you told me to do."

"What does that matter? Get on with your work and don't
stand talking to me."

"Do you mean to say that I've got to go on doing what I've
already done?"

"That's part of the punishment," he said.

That conversation has always remained in my mind as
typifying the attitude of those who run our prison system.
The authorities looked upon prison as punitive and still do,
in spite of minor alterations for the better since that time,
such as the abolition of broad arrows, the addition of golden

WE SHALL NOT CEASE

syrup, and a small quantity of dripping* in the diet (and I am told if you have golden syrup you can't have dripping and vice versa) and an increase in the amount of bread. Such being the system, it is impossible for the warders who carry it out to do anything but rule by fear and be ruled themselves by fear— fear of their charges and fear of spying and reporting which prevails among the staff.

On the second evening, I was put into another cell in a different part of the building. This cell had a drainpipe in a corner, covered with a grating, and a hammock instead of a mattress. Not being accustomed to hammocks, I put all the blankets on top of me as the night was cold. During the night I awoke with my back like a sheet of ice and found that the drainpipe was directing a shaft of cold air right onto it. I put blankets underneath, but, as it turned out, I was already too late. Towards the evening of the next day I felt hot and at the same time shivered, and my back ached. During the night I grew worse, and in the morning when I tried to rise, I was too sick and giddy to stand and had to get back into the hammock. After a while the warder came in.

"Come on, you've got to get up."

"I can't. I'm too ill."

"Well, I don't know what to do about it," he said. "I'd better go and see."

He returned with the information that he supposed I'd better stay there. Then he went out, slamming and locking the door behind him. For days I lay there without attention of any kind, wretchedly ill, in the extreme of physical and mental misery. I would see the walls closing in on me and fight them off desperately. They would melt away and I would swing right out into space. When my head was clear enough for me to be aware of my condition and surroundings, I was even worse off. The pain in my back was frightful. I was

*Fat.

constantly sick, and I was forced at frequent intervals to pass, with excruciating pain, a small quantity of blood and pus. I was very thirsty, but there was only the tea to drink and that I could not touch. The ordinary prison meals were put in at regular intervals and removed untouched. Occasionally one of the warders came in and I asked for a doctor, but in vain. One of them looked at the contents of the tin.

"What's all this blood and stuff?" he asked.

"That's my urine."

"By jove, you're in a bad way."

But nothing was done for me.

After five or six days the fever left me, though the other symptoms remained, and I managed to take a little porridge. The warder came in and ordered me to get up and accompany him. "You're going before the doctor," he said.

I went with him, hardly able to keep on my legs from weakness, and bent with the pain in my back, but buoyed up with the hope that I should now get some treatment. In the office were the stern Chief Warder, a man in civilian clothes sitting at the other side of the room looking at papers, and the doctor who had examined me at the Barracks.

✠ ✠ ✠

The Chief Warder followed me into the passage and shouted at me: "Stand up straight and walk properly! None of that slouching! We don't allow it here!"

I was too utterly crushed to attempt to defend myself. Completely in the hands of men who were determined to show me neither justice nor mercy, I saw not one ray of hope. The warder took me back to the hall outside my cell and told me to scrub the floor.

"I can't," I said. "It's not that I'm not willing to. I really can't."

"I know that," he answered, "but I can't let you off. I'll have to report you to the Governor for refusing to work."

I wondered what would happen. I would be punished, I supposed, and how was I going to stand punishment in such a condition?

When he took me, later, back to the office, the doctor had gone; only the man in civilian clothes was there and with him the Chief Warder. The warder who had brought me made his report, and finished up with: "He looks a pretty sick man to me, sir."

"And to me, too," said the Governor. "Give him a spell for a few days and then we can see."

Only a few words, but they were spoken kindly, and they made all the difference to me. I went back to my cell a different being, with faith and hope and strength for the future springing up anew.

Health came slowly back, and in those days of complete idleness I had plenty of opportunity for thinking matters over. What would happen to me I could not foretell, but that the path before me would not be an easy one, I had very little doubt. Come what might, I hoped I would be given the strength to go through with it.

It was Easter time. On the Sunday, a Catholic choir came into the prison and sang. The hymns of joy and inspiration floating through that abode of misery, seemed to me, lying in my cell, like angel voices, and my spirit was lifted up above pain and weakness to union with all the aspirations and ideals of man at one in God.

A few days later the warder asked me if I felt up to a little work.

"Do just as much as you like," he said, "and no matter how little it is, I won't say anything."

After my illness most of the warders showed me what little kindness they could, which was not much, as the seniors spied on the juniors, and the juniors on one another, and they all knew that the discovery of the slightest leniency towards a prisoner meant a report. Hence anything in the way of kindness or friendliness had to be clandestine.

It was very little I could do at first, but gradually my strength came back. The Governor, passing on his rounds, stopped and spoke to me. "How are you getting on, Baxter? Feeling better?"

"I'm very much better, thank you."

"You're not finding the work too hard?"

"No, not now."

"I'm very pleased to see you better and getting on all right," he said. "You had a rough time, but I did my best for you and I hope you will soon be quite well."

He spoke as man to man and not as jailer to prisoner. He made me feel an ordinary human being with an individuality again, a feeling one is apt to lose in the routine of prison. Moreover, seeing and talking to a man who was not in uniform was a relief to the eye and the mind.

I thoroughly served my apprenticeship in scrubbing and cleaning. I scrubbed cells, corridors, and halls. Every day I soaked and scrubbed the boards I had soaked and scrubbed the day before. The cells in that damp, sunless place never got a chance to dry properly from one day to another. If by any chance the boards did look dry by the afternoon when the Chief Warder made his rounds, this was regarded as proving that they had not been properly cleaned, and I was told to use more water. I protested at the futility of it and the unwholesomeness, but of course fruitlessly.

Scrubbing out the next cell to mine, I found it less damp and rather better lighted, owing to its position, than the one I inhabited. Moreover, it had a mattress instead of a hammock, which I thought would be an advantage to me with my sore back. As a matter of fact the mattress needed airing; lying as they did on the floors that were never quite dry, they were all more or less damp all the time. I approached the warder with a suggestion that I should move into it as it was empty. He looked in and agreed that it was better. "Move in, and I'll say I told you to shift."

When my card, giving my name and particulars, was shifted, I noticed that I was down as "agnostic." "Who put that down?" I asked the warder indignantly.

"You must have given it in your particulars when you came in."

"I said I didn't belong to any organized Church. That's not to say I'm an agnostic. I'm not, and you can take that down."

To my surprise he did so. Evidently one had the freedom of one's religion in prison. I asked him what he thought agnostic meant, and he said: "A man who doesn't believe in God or Devil."

The space for religion remained a blank, but not for long. The following Sunday I was ordered to join the Catholic squad on its way to service.

"But I'm not a Catholic."

"Yes, you are, it's on your card." And it was. My predecessor in the cell had been a Catholic, and the hymn book and book of devotions he had used were still on the shelf. I had found them very interesting and had objected to giving them up. Seeing this, the prison authorities, greatly worried about the blank on my card, had thankfully put down "Roman Catholic."

Most of the political* were labeled "agnostic," as I found when I happened to be near their cells on the upper landing. They wore their own clothes, did no work, and exercised apart. It was not easy to obtain speech with them, since they came out of the yard before we went in, but occasionally I managed to snatch a few minutes. The political wheel

*Unionist and Labour leaders who were imprisoned for their left-wing beliefs.

has made a complete revolution in New Zealand since those days, and some of those men are now members of the government.

Once I was fit again I did not find the work very hard, but some of the casuals, usually in for fourteen days for drunkenness or the like offenses, had a rough time. The warders were always hard on newcomers, shouted at them, bullied them, and harassed them until they had them thoroughly cowed and amenable to the discipline of the place. The casuals never got beyond that first stage. They were often in a poor state of health, recovering from a drunken bout, or "without lawful means of support" because they had neither the mental nor the physical stamina to do steady work. I did my best to show them the right way of doing things, and they were very grateful for the assistance, but they found that they were still shouted at and bullied, no matter what they did or how hard they tried to do things the right way. There were some who took it quite calmly.

"Put some elbow grease into it," a warder said to one of them.

"I'm doing my best," he replied. "A man can't do any more, can he?"

"Use your holystone," said the warder.

"My what?"

"Your holystone."

"You've got me," he said with a resigned air of bewilderment, sitting back with a scrubbing brush in his hand.

One poor old wreck roused my sympathy. He had got fourteen days for sleeping in a shed on his way into the country, having been warned to clear out of the town within twenty-four hours. He was manifestly unequal to the task he had to perform, and, having finished the job I was on, I offered to do it for him. He leaned against the wall while I scrubbed, and we talked. Unfortunately we neglected to keep a lookout and the warder caught us. He directed a stream of abuse at the old man, who seized his brush in terror. I explained that it was my fault, that I had offered to do it for him.

"He knows right enough what he's not allowed to do," said the warder.

The last I saw of the old man, he was scrubbing for dear life under the eye of the angry warder.

I came to know a good many of the other prisoners at work and on exercise. An old Scotchman, whose books had failed to pass muster at the time of his bankruptcy, warned me on no account to ask anyone what he was in for.

"You'll get something frightful if you do," he said, "and often not the truth at all."

Nevertheless, I heard a good many unsolicited stories. Several told me they were innocent of the crimes they had been sentenced for, and in some cases I found it hard not to believe them. One man in particular was very convincing. He had had a shop, and one day the small child of a customer, known to him, wandered into the shop. He took her hand to lead her to her home, only a short distance away. On the way they met two women who recognized the child, and said that he was taking her to a vacant section across the street and only turned back when he saw them. They afterwards admitted that he hadn't even left the pavement to cross the street when they first saw him. But the police searched his premises and found some indecent postcards, and that, he said, finished him.

"I haven't led a good life," he said. "I haven't been right with women. I admit that. But touch a child! Me! Never! And the funny thing was, the judge was on my side. He said he didn't understand how the jury could have convicted on the evidence, and he gave me a light sentence, only nine months, and here I am."

Some, on the other hand, were quite ready to admit their

crimes and their interest centered on their own sentences and the crimes and sentences of others. One remarkable-looking individual with one eye was awaiting trial for robbery with violence. He had held up a man in the street with a revolver.

"The revolver was no good," he said, "and wouldn't shoot. But he wasn't to know that. Didn't John Fat flinch and tremble when I pointed it at him! It was worth my sentence to see his jaw drop."

He asked me what sentence I thought he'd get.

"Judging by other cases," I said, "I should think you'd get ten years."

"I think it'll be fourteen," he said. "Threatening to shoot; they always give it hot for that."

A man came into the yard after his sentence had been pronounced, and burst into tears.

"Four bloody years," he wailed over and over again. "Four bloody years."

The others were angry at this fuss; they had worries enough of their own.

"What's four years?" they said. "You ought to do it on your head."

The savage sentences that were given a few decades ago are fortunately no longer so common. There were men in the Terrace doing as much as fourteen years for certain offenses, such as homosexuality. That there was also a certain amount of it in prison, I believe, but not nearly as much as the warders suspected.

One day I was placed by the warder just round the corner from the bathroom, to await my turn in the bath. He went away for a moment and the man ahead of me called out: "You can come in now; I'm ready."

I went to the door and found him just finishing dressing. The warder came rushing back.

"What do you mean, going away from where I put you! Don't you know two men are not allowed in the bathroom together?"

"How can you expect me to obey the regulations when you won't let me read them?" I asked.

But he stormed on. "I could put you up for this. Going into the bathroom when there's another man there is counted as being taken in the act."

I was thoroughly sickened and disgusted.

"What's all this fuss about two men being together in the bathroom?" I asked the other prisoners.

"Just because there are one or two crazy men here," they said, "the rest of us decent chaps have to put up with treatment like that. That screw's had trouble when he's been in charge, so he's always on the lookout for it."

In the large majority of cases such precautions were not justified, and their application to everyone resulted in a lowering of self-respect.

We were always searched when we came in from exercise. The coat was handed to the warder, who looked through it, then ran his hands over one's body. One evening, as we came in, four names were called out in my section, my own amongst them. Each man of the four, as he came to his cell door, remained standing beside it instead of going in. When my turn came I stood in the doorway and removed my clothes until I was stark naked, throwing each article one by one to the warder waiting in the corridor. He went through them carefully. Then he came into the cell.

"Open your mouth. Raise your arms. That'll do. Now lean forward and spread your legs."

He passed round behind me. When I realized what he was doing I said: "That's a pretty disgusting thing to put on to a man."

"Yes, it is," he replied, unexpectedly, "and I hate doing it to a man like you. I won't do it to you again if I can help it. Don't think that any of us like it. We all hate doing it."

"I'm sure you do," I said.

The next time my name was called he kept his word, and when he came into the cell, merely stood in front of me for a moment with a smile, then went out.

The senior warder in charge immediately shouted: "You haven't searched that man properly! You haven't had time."

He came into the cell. "Did he search you properly?" he asked.

"Certainly," I said.

"I don't believe either of you," he remarked, with some justification. "This time I'll let it pass, but you won't get away with it again."

When the next time came I had to stand in the doorway of the cell while the warder examined me under the eyes of his superior.

"He beat you that time," I remarked to him afterwards.

"No damn fear," he said, "I kept my eyes shut."

Many of the prisoners complained of a lack of sex feeling. One would have thought this would have been an advantage, in a place where they saw no woman from year's end to year's end; but they strongly resented it and were unanimous in putting it down to dope in the tea. Nothing could shake this conviction. "I know them," they'd say, with the queer overexcitement characteristic of them, resulting, partly at least, from the constant repression. Certainly the strange appearance and taste of the tea lent some color to the theory.

They were full of theories, always to do with prison life or police-court proceedings that were so closely connected with it. One man told me that when autumn came and the prison gardens all over the country needed expert manuring and treatment, a number of Chinese were always rounded up and given long enough sentences to enable the work to be done.

"No nonsense about it," he said when I laughed, "and it's coming close to the time now, you'll see."

Strangely enough, about ten days later, several Chinese appeared in the prison.

The interests of the men, naturally enough, centered round the petty gossip of the prison. They had nothing else to occupy their minds or to break the monotony of existence. Completely cut off from ordinary life and doing everything under orders and nothing that was not ordered, all initiative was slowly sapped, even in thought. Nothing was done to encourage them to organize amongst themselves for concerts or games. Now, I believe, interested people from outside give concerts and lectures at intervals, and others start men on suitable courses of study, providing the necessary books for them. But even now, I do not think there is any organization for recreation within the prison. Not in Mt. Eden at any rate. When I was in the Terrace little or no interest was taken in the prisoners by the outside world, and of recreation they had absolutely none. Many of them were not readers and could not concentrate on a book for any length of time. They had no guidance in the choice of books. The library was a poor one and the librarian was chosen, not for his knowledge of books, but for his smartness in patching and re-covering them. It was small wonder that in the dreary monotony of their life the prisoners found amusement in childish and petty behavior. The making of obscene noises was the favorite diversion, rendered all the more exciting by the notice the warders took of it. I attended the Anglican service one Sunday, after having extracted an assurance that I would not be compelled to attend every Sunday thereafter if I did not wish to. An aged clergyman conducted the service, and preached a sermon as far removed from the needs and diffi-culties of his congregation as anything could well be. A loud, explosive noise was heard. The warders rushed at a man a few places from me and dragged him out of the chapel, amid loud shouts from him of "I didn't do it, you've got the wrong man this time," and answering shouts from them of "Well, tell us who did it, then." The aged clergyman took not the faintest notice and went serenely on with his sermon. It would have been better if the warders had done the same. We listened to the gradually receding bangs, thuds, and shouts, which went on outside the door.

"And did they get the wrong man?" I asked the others afterwards.

"You bet they didn't; it was him all right. He's a champion at it!"

The same noise would also be heard after the men were locked in their cells for the night. It was not easy for the warders to trace it, and no doubt the champion got the blame, sometimes unjustly.

I was told that punching and battering went on when men were being taken to the punishment cells. I never witnessed anything of the kind myself, but that is not to say it did not happen when men put up any resistance, as they sometimes did. To make a complaint against a warder was doomed to failure from the start. According to the regulations, which I did in the end manage to memorize, if a prisoner considered that an order given him by a warder was not justified, he was to obey the order immediately, but was allowed to make a complaint to the authorities. If he failed to substantiate his complaint, he was deemed to have made a frivolous complaint, and he was punished. In actual fact, no prisoner could make anything but a frivolous complaint, as his word was never taken against a warder's and the only witnesses he could bring were prisoners too. The only successful complaint that I ever heard of was when, a little while before I arrived in the prison, nearly all the prisoners combined to complain of the staleness of the bread. Stale bread, when it has to be eaten dry as the sole article of food at a meal, is not very attractive. The consequence of this most unusual solidarity was that when I was there the bread arrived for tea damp and smoking. As it was usually consumed then and there its effect on the digestions of men who ate it every night for years on end, and remained in their cells for the night afterwards, can hardly have been good. In prison one can hardly ever get the men to stand together for anything and it is this characteristic that makes it easy to rule by fear.

One night I was awakened by blood-curdling yells. I leapt out of bed before I realized that if there was a tragedy I was prevented by the locked door from doing anything. It was a terrific uproar. Stentorian shouts at the top of a powerful voice, of: "I am Jesus Christ, the Son of God!" Then more yells and scufflings and bumpings and shouts from the warders. By this time I had come to the conclusion, which was correct, that it was a drunk in the D.T.s. The sounds continued for some time, then gradually died away.

Next morning the warder called me out. I followed him along to the padded cell. Instead of the usual spy-hole in the door, it had a hole nearly large enough to admit a man's head. The principal warder in charge approached his face to the opening. Immediately the fist of the occupant shot out, catching him between the eyes and laying him on the broad of his back. There was a rush of warders to the door and the man was dragged out attired only in his shirt, a mass of filth from head to foot. They handcuffed him and ran him down the passage to the bathroom. I went into his cell.

"Have I really got to clean this?" I asked the warder. "Come and look."

He stepped in. Walls, floor, and even ceiling were plastered with filth. "Isn't it something awful! But it's got to be cleaned so you'll have to get on with it. You can get it off the ceiling with a mop."

Several days later, passing by, I saw the man standing in the door of the padded cell, completely naked, catching lice.

"Not enough light in there to see them," he remarked to me.

He was a good physical specimen, tall and well built. His nakedness was not obtrusive as he was covered from head to foot with a fell of reddish silky hair. The card over his door stated: "Remanded for medical attention," and beneath that, "4s. 6d." I asked him: "Have you seen the doctor?"

"No," he said.

I asked some of the others about it.

They said, "He may have had some dope shot into him the night he came in."

The four and six, they told me, was the fee, at the rate of one and six a day. It would be added on to his fine when he went before the court. I have only his word and theirs for this.

There were men in prison who were obviously mentally unbalanced, not just subnormal or mentally deficient, as quite a number were, but actually of unsound mind. In one case especially I was struck with the cruelty of keeping the man there in such a condition. He was a man of some education, had been a lawyer's clerk or something of the kind. He held forth continually on his wrongs and on the injustice of his case, using much legal phraseology. He was blind and I was told that in his anger and desperation he had destroyed his own eyesight. He was in a wretched condition, unable to feed himself properly or to keep himself or his cell clean. Even if the warders had had time or opportunity to help him, he fell into such a state of rage and excitement if they came near him that they usually left him to himself and to the filth that, unaided, he got into.

With the other prisoners he did not get on much better. Many of them were too full of their own miseries to take the trouble to show him friendliness, and there were some who teased and annoyed him, driving him to frenzy. He responded, however, to the least attempt at kindness or sympathy and would let me lead him in the yard and clean up his cell which was in a frightful mess as he spilt everything. The warders were thankful to find anyone who would attend to him and I was allowed to do what I could for him.

A man whom I had often seen in the streets, propelling himself in a wheelchair, was serving a sentence while I was in the Terrace. His legs were shriveled and atrophied—quite useless. As he could not have his chair in prison he had to drag himself about on his hands and feet. His hands had hard pads from constant walking on them.

One day I saw clay on the floor of the passage I had lately scrubbed. This meant that someone had come over from Mt. Cook prison. The prisoners at the Terrace never had dirty boots. One of the other cleaners told me a man had just been brought over for punishment. "He's in that cell."

I went over and looked through the spy hole. The man was like some trapped wild animal, his eyes glaring, his whole appearance expressing desperation and defiance. I rattled the spy hole shutter and whispered: "Got any tobacco?"

"No," suspiciously.

"Like some?"

"Too right, I would."

He came up to the door, human again, his face relaxed from his fierce revolt. I got him a piece of tobacco from the library where I knew the librarian had a store secreted, and pushed it through the hole.

A few days later one of the warders called me from my work. "Come along. I've got a job for you; you're to come and talk to a man in the dummy.* Wait a minute; I'd better search you; we don't want you to be taking him tobacco."

The ceremony over, I asked him: "Do you always do this when a man's in the dummy?"

---

*Solitary confinement.

"When he's in for fourteen days. We're not supposed to let him go the whole time without someone to talk to. He might go batty."

We went down stairways until we were well below the level of the ground. The warder unlocked a door and we came into a small enclosed passage with a door opening into it.

"This is where he takes his exercise," he said, unlocking the other door. "You go in here: I'll be back for you after a while," and he locked me in.

The punishment cell was a cement box, without a stick of furniture in it; nothing to sit on but the concrete floor. At night the inmate could get his blankets, but in the daytime he had nothing. There seemed to be no opening in it, but some sort of outlet to the passage there must have been, for there was sufficient light for me to make out the face of the occupant, who was the man I had given tobacco to a few days before. His defensive hostility melted almost immediately and he was soon pouring out all his bottled-up resentment against the injustice of his treatment. His sense of his wrongs prevented him from submitting quietly to jail discipline, and raised a whole host of new wrongs to fight against. He told me that he should not have been in jail at all. "I've not done anything different from what thousands of men like me do every day and nobody thinks of putting them in jail and I'm here."

He had gone, he said, to a picnic with a girl who had taken him and other men, too, many times before. They had gone away from the others. Suddenly, people, strangers, had come upon them. To save the situation for herself the girl had screamed and there was a great uproar.

"Not that I blame the girl, mind you. She didn't mean to send me to jail, but once she'd told her story she had to stick to it. Up I went as high as a kite and got eighteen months for indecent assault."

Coming to jail with a well-established grievance, the whole system had appeared to him as another grievance and he fought it all the time. He had had an argument with a warder at Mt. Cook.

"I was in the right and the screw knew it, but d'you think he'd say so? Not him, and his word was taken against mine, so I threw down my shovel and here I am."

I admired his pluck, but it seemed pretty hopeless and I said so. Most men were done after fourteen days on bread and water in the dummy, though even in the short time I was at the Terrace I knew a man who was not. He got another fourteen days on top of it. He was done then.

We argued over the pros and cons of fighting jail authorities on one's own. I didn't see that he could help his case by making things hard for himself in prison. It went rather against the grain to advise him to act expediently rather than on principle, but it seemed the best way out for him, and hadn't I done it to a certain extent? I was obeying orders in prison and I had come there on a military sentence. My illness had come on me before I had thought the matter out.

We talked until the opening door showed that time was up.

"You've done me good," he said. "I'll think over what you said."

Outside, the warder asked me: "How did you get on?"

"All right; he seems a decent sort of chap."

"I wouldn't be left alone with him for a good deal," he said.

"And yet you'd lock me in with him!"

"That's quite different. He wouldn't touch you."

They ruled by fear and were afraid of the men they ruled. And yet those men who fought against the system were not always the worst, by any means. There was often more hope of the man whom the authorities would call "one of the worst men here" than of the "good" prisoner, who was often subnormal and who, obedient and well-behaved under orders, was quite incapable of looking after himself in the normal life of the community.

There were a number of prisoners on remand at the Terrace. They did not exercise with us, but actually we had plenty of opportunity of mixing with them. Two boys, brothers, came in on a charge of stealing a sheep. The younger must have been fifteen, but he did not look more than twelve. In the daytime, when he was with his brother, he managed to stand up to it and keep a brave face to the world. But at night, locked up alone in his cell, his control gave way and he wailed and sobbed far into the night. The desolate sounds, echoing through the empty corridors, tore at the nerves of prisoners and warders alike.

"What's the matter?" a warder called through the door at the boy.

"Oh, my heart is broken."

"Well, stop that noise or it'll be more than your heart'll be broken if I have to come in to you."

He'd stop for a while and then break out again, uncontrollably.

Very different were three boys of about the same age, convicted of car conversion* and on their way to Borstal.† Bright-faced, high-spirited boys of a good type, they never allowed anyone to see them or hear them without the shield of pluck they held up, whatever lay behind it. The principal warder in our section read them a lecture, to which they listened respectfully. They were not to consider themselves criminals or to lose their self-respect. They were merely being sent to where they would be taught to behave. I wondered how they would fare in the Borstal. Would it be cells, warders, and prison routine or would there really be a different system of development instead of repression?

---

*Car theft.
†Reform school.

One afternoon, on exercise, I saw Mark Briggs. I knew him, for I had had him pointed out to me when we were at the Barracks. He was walking in the second offenders' yard, barred off from us lest he should corrupt us on his return from Trentham with a second sentence of hard labor. With me in the first offenders' yard were men doing life for murder and men doing long sentences for crimes of violence and perversion. And Briggs might corrupt them! Red tape run riot! I managed to exchange a few words with him at the gap in the barrier.

"Anyone who takes a second dose of this is a glutton," I said.

"Does that mean you'd throw it in rather than face a second go?"

I hastened to explain that I hadn't meant that at all, but was merely amused at seeing him in the second offenders' yard. He passed on to Mt. Cook and for the time being I saw him no more.

I was not anxious for the change to Mt. Cook, which, I supposed, would come when someone, perhaps the Governor, considered me fit for the work there. I had become accustomed to the routine at the Terrace and knew the worst that could happen to me there. Whereas Mt. Cook I didn't know and I had heard lurid accounts, from prisoners sent over to the Terrace for punishment, of the hard work over there, of a brick kiln in which you were baked alive and the soles of your boots curled up with the heat. I thought that, not being up to my usual strength, I might find the work too hard.

However, what I thought on the matter was not likely to affect the course of events. In due time I found myself sitting on the back of a lorry on my way to Mt. Cook. It was pleasant, anyway, to be out in the fresh air again and see hills and the harbor down below me and hear the ordinary street sounds, after having been completely cut off from them for weeks, although I could not help being self-conscious in my conspicuous attire. The thought of escape did pass through my mind, for the driver never turned his head, and I could easily have slipped off when the lorry was going slowly; but the broad arrows would have put it out of the question, even if I had had any real thoughts of escaping, and I had not. I had made up my mind on that matter long before.

The lorry ran up to the gates of the prison, passing a group of men shoveling out clay from the hillside with an armed guard over them. I recognized several of them, my brothers amongst them.

The warder who received me said I must have another pair of boots; the ones I had worn at the Terrace were not strong enough for outside work. I tried on a pair.

"No good. I'd go lame in five minutes in these."

They brought me several pairs and I rejected them all. Finally, the warder took me up to the stores. Trying on all these boots had given me the illusion of being in a shoe shop, and it was with a distinct jar that I heard the warder say to the man in charge of the stores: "Here's a prisoner can't get fitted for boots. See if you can fix him up with a pair."

A prisoner! Well, I knew I was, but I never felt like one, and as it happened in the Terrace I had always been referred to as "this man" or "Baxter."

I tried on pair after pair. Dreadful boots, impossible boots, all apparently made for men with feet as broad as they were long, and mine are long and narrow. When I did get anything to fit in length there were inches to spare in width. Moreover, they were all out of shape and had bumps and ridges in the most unexpected places. At last they brought out a new pair and these I accepted in some triumph.

Next, I had an interview with Burrows, who was in charge of Mt. Cook. The two prisons were run in conjunction, under one superintendent.

Burrows was very reasonable. He asked me whether

I looked on my sentence as military or civil. I said as it had been imposed by a court-martial, I would regard it as military.

"That's so, but once you are handed over to the civil authorities, you are entirely in our hands. The military authorities have nothing more to do with you as long as you are here. So you won't object to working as it won't be under military orders."

I saw that he had probably had trouble with the others and wished I could have spoken with them first, but that, of course, was what he wanted to prevent. I said that as I had worked at the Terrace I did not see that I could refuse to work now. He seemed relieved. He always endeavored to avoid trouble, often compromising when another man might have been unyielding, in order that things might go smoothly. Offenses against discipline were fairly common at Mt. Cook, and men were often sent over to the Terrace for punishment, but I don't think it was due to greater leniency. Most of the prisoners at Mt. Cook were short-sentence men, who as a rule, were less amenable to discipline than the men who had been in prison longer, having retained some spirit. They looked much healthier than the men in the Terrace.

I found a considerable difference between the two prisons. The work, for one thing, was nearly all in the open air. I worked in a gang with my mates. The cells, owing to the fact that the building was of lighter structure, were much airier and admitted more light, especially where we were, on the upper landing, on which the cells had skylights instead of windows. We washed in the hall instead of our cells, and, consequently, never had time to wash properly as the warder's whistle always went before we could possibly have finished and we had to stop immediately and go back to our cells. The bread ration was larger—sixteen ounces instead of twelve—and so was the meat ration.

There was one warder at Mt. Cook who thought my pride needed taking down a peg—my overweening pride that was such a trouble to officers in the army. At least a dozen times, I am sure, in the six weeks, he made me strip naked for search. He succeeded in making me very angry, but not in taking down my pride. I very nearly revolted, but only refrained because I had so little time to go.

When I joined my friends in the clay-cutting gang I was heartily welcomed. No one seemed to have hit on illness as the reason I had been left behind at the Terrace, and as I was by now pretty well again I don't think they believed there had been much the matter with me. Many of these men I had known at the Barracks. Some of them I met for the first time. My new boots came in for admiration and envy. Did I think they could get new ones too? I thought it very unlikely, since they had put up for weeks with the ones they had.

As I had thought, my brothers and Little had doubted when they first came over whether they should work in prison, but Burrows had explained to them carefully that they were entirely under civil control, and they had taken it on, though rather doubtfully.

The work was not hard for men accustomed to manual labor, and Jack and I, at least, soon found that we had to accommodate ourselves to a much slower pace than anything we had been accustomed to. Once we forgot ourselves and went on shoveling clay into the trucks with such vigor that the man who drove the trucks to the brick yard came back with a strongly worded message that we were to moderate our stroke; they couldn't keep up with what we were doing. Some of our lot, who were unused to work of that kind, didn't make a very good showing. One man, who had worked in a shop, used to get hold of a ridiculous little shovel that had somehow got amongst the others, which hardly lifted more than a spoonful of clay. The warder would say: "There's

Hugh got that shovel again," and take it from him, but he nearly always managed to get it back.

I recognized several familiar faces amongst the civil prisoners. A Maori, who had been waiting his turn in the office when I had my memorable interview with the doctor, said to me with a friendly smile: "Glad to see you well again. When I see you last, you just one inch from the peg hole."

One of our group told me hair-raising tales of the crimes he had heard of since he had come to prison—crimes he had never known existed. He pointed out the Maori as having committed a particularly bestial crime. I said I didn't believe it. He was not that sort, and anyway, I had heard something quite different about him.

"Who told you?"

"He did."

"Did you ask him?"

He admitted he had. I said that that was what he could expect to get if he asked. They had feelings and would fire out that kind of thing as a sort of defense. But I don't think he believed me.

There were men there who had committed horrible crimes. There is a great deal of difference between crimes that are really horrible and crimes that are made to appear so by law. Words can hypnotize people. Nothing exemplifies this better than the phrase "Habitual Criminal." It conjures up a picture of incorrigible rascality and marks out the possessor of its brand as a being of a different species from his fellows. Even amongst the prisoners this was the case. I have had a man pointed out to me.

"Do you see that man? He's just been declared an habitual criminal."

As if the man in question had suddenly become something entirely different from themselves. And what does it really mean? That a man, convicted of an indictable offense a certain number of times, has been declared by the judge who tried his case to be an habitual criminal under the Act, the Dog Act,* as it was called in prison. Some judges would frequently make use of the act, others never at all. Having been declared an H.C., a man could be—and often was—upon the expiration of his definite sentence, detained in prison until the Prisons Board, which as a general rule means the jail officials, saw fit to release him. And even then the brand is still upon the man, and the indefinite sentence can come into operation again if he is reconvicted, the judge of course being aware of it, and the jury, too, in many cases, with the result that a conviction is certain on the sketchiest evidence. Men have no right of appeal against that sentence, no means of breaking out of the trap that holds them.

The habitual criminals I knew in prison were filled with bitterness and despair at the hopelessness of ever freeing themselves or being freed from the grasp of the Act. I was particularly sorry for one man. A kind-hearted, decent little chap, his trouble was drink, and he had frequent convictions for using obscene language when silly with it. For this he had been declared an H.C. and was being held for an indefinite period in prison.

He said to me: "You've been one of us; you know the life we lead here, better than anyone outside can ever know it. Do something for us when you get out. People will listen to you. They won't listen to us. Try to get the H.C. Act altered. We're helpless and can do nothing for ourselves. Don't forget us."

I have not forgotten them, but my influence on the legislators of the country has been negative rather than positive and I can only work indirectly by influencing others.

Often men worked themselves into a state of nervous excitement at the prospect of approaching release. One unfortunate man, who was to be released in three months

*Habitual Criminals and Offenders Act of 1906, similar to "three strikes you're out."

time, became so worked up about it that he could bear it no longer and, the opportunity offering, he escaped. We could see him for a long time running up the road that led to the hills, his clothes making him a conspicuous mark. Recapture was inevitable and in a short time he was back amongst us with a year to serve instead of three months.

All prisoners, at the conclusion of the first three months of their sentences, were allowed to smoke on exercise. But we, having only a three months sentence to serve, were not allowed to smoke at all. Many of our gang were not smokers and the deprivation meant nothing to them. Though I was only a light smoker when I came to prison, I found the craving much stronger than it had ever been before and very hard to withstand. A tobacco allowance was sometimes put into my cell by mistake and as I couldn't smoke it I chewed it, as most of the other prisoners did, for their time for legitimate smoking was short. Sometimes I, and others too, risked smoking in my cell. It was a big risk, of course. One night I had just lit up, when there was a shout of "Someone smoking!" in the passage. I hurriedly put it out, hid it, and waited for my door to open. It did not, but some other unfortunate's did, and I heard him being removed from his cell with the usual accompanying din. But attempts at smoking were necessarily few and far between. I chewed and the habit called down many rebukes from my fellow objectors. What filthy habits I had picked up in jail!

We talked together on exercise and we talked at work, too, within limits, and in my opinion we talked far too much on the everlasting subject of what would be done with us. Our business was to stand out against military service, come what might.

The consequence did not concern us and endless speculations on them did no good. But that fact did not stop the speculations.

3

THE TIME CAME when the sentences of Little, my brothers, and myself, expired, and we were taken over to the Terrace. As we passed the stairway to the upper tier, there was a shout from above and the face of the one-eyed highway robber appeared over the landing rails, "Hullo, Baxie," he called. "You were right, I got ten years."

"Nice friends you seem to have made here," said the others. When we were in the reception office getting back our clothes, Jack remarked: "We're not going out; we've liked it so much here were going to stay."

The Chief Warder was there and several others. I hardly think any of the Irish warders could have been there. They believed him.

"You can't stay here when your time is up," boomed the Chief. "We'll put you out."

"Oh yes, we can," I chipped in. "We'll make a disturbance when we're put out and we'll be arrested and come straight back in here."

It must have been with intense relief that they saw us depart with our military escort, making, in spite of our threats, no attempt to get back in again.

We were marched to the Barracks at the other end of Wellington. After a few hours there we were marched back again through the town to the railway station. Hard on any army footwear, as well as on our own, but useful in accustoming us to bear the public eye in circumstances that would once have been humiliating.

At Trentham we found we were regarded in the light of heroes by soldiers, prisoners, and guards alike. "These men have been to jail," was said, almost with bated breath. The time had not yet come when hundreds of men, passing from camp to jail, had made the thing a commonplace. We were the pioneers.

The same procedure was gone through as before. Offered our kits; refused them; sentenced to twenty-eight days detention for refusing them. There was one innovation. A paper was brought with a name signed at the end of it. The signature was shown to me.

"Is that your signature?"

"Yes. I think it's mine. It looks very like it."

They opened the paper and showed me my name appended to the attestation paper, with a declaration that I was willing to fight in any part of the Empire. I knew I had never signed any such statement, but there was my signature, exactly as I was accustomed to make it. There was a space for witnesses, left blank.

"Where are the witnesses' names?" I asked. "If I had signed, the witnesses would have signed, too."

They had evidently overlooked the necessity for putting in the witnesses names, and gave it up. Nevertheless they continued to declare I had signed it.

When we arrived back at the Barracks after another march through Wellington, we found the same changed atmosphere.

"You chaps not taking on anything?" said the guards, and I

am sure they would have been very disappointed if we had said we were. "You'd like something to eat? It's late, but we'll manage to get you a cup of tea."

There were many new faces. Teachers, clerks, farmers, workers, of all shades of opinion, united in their opposition to military service. I met many men that I should have liked to know better, but the opportunity was not given me.

We had written home, but no news had so far reached us of what was happening to the other members of the family. So that it was a complete surprise to me when one evening I looked down from the top-story landing and saw my brother Donald far below. He waved and shouted up to me that Hugh was with him. He disappeared then into some region out of my sight. I went back to Jack with the news in some excitement.

"That means they're both started on our track," he said, and we looked forward to hearing all about it in the morning.

But we did not. Early, before the other prisoners were out of their cells, Little, Jack, Sandy, and I were taken down to the entrance and handed over to an escort of military police. Once again, and now for the last time, we were marched through the streets of Wellington. I came last of the four and the guard walking behind me kept deliberately treading on my heels. At last I stopped.

"If you don't leave off doing that," I said, "I'll refuse to move a step."

I had rightly concluded that they did not want a disturbance and he gave it up. I had a pretty good idea of our destination, and when we came to the entrance to the wharves I saw I had been right. As we turned down to the gates an individual leaning against the wall of the pub at the corner called out: "Why did you wait 'til you've got to be taken?"

The transport *Waitemata* lay at one of the wharves and we were pushed up her gangway and down into the clink. It already had ten occupants. Seven we knew: They had been with us at Mt. Cook. Sanderson, a religious objector, had been brought from the Terrace, and two Irishmen, Maguire and Kirwan, from Trentham. This made the number up to fourteen.* We represented varying viewpoints: A member of the sect "Testimony of Jesus," a pacifist Catholic, a member of the Labour Party, and an Irishman who wouldn't fight for the British because of what had lately happened in Ireland. These were a few examples of the different attitudes from which we came to our stand. One thing was noticeable about the experimental fourteen. Almost without exception we were drawn from the ranks of the proletariat, and the exceptions were known to be opponents of the government. We were chosen for our obscurity, being thought unlikely ever to make our protests heard either personally or through our relatives.

The clink measured, roughly, twenty feet by ten. It had two tiers of bunks running round it and portholes on the outside. A small cabin opened out of it at one end with a porthole and a ventilator shaft leading into it from the deck above. The only entrance to the clink was through the isolation ward.

No communication had been allowed with relatives or friends, but some of the earlier arrivals had thrown letters out on to the wharf in the hope that they would be picked up by the waterside workers, who had expressed sympathy when they saw us being forcibly taken on board, and forwarded to their destinations. By this means word did reach some of the families of the deported men, but not, of course, until after all hope of seeing them was past.

The *Waitemata* sailed early in the afternoon.† We were hardly out of the harbor before we ran into dirty weather. A

---

*The fourteen were: Frederick Adin, Garth Ballantyne, the Baxter brothers—Archibald, Alexander (Sandy), John (Jack)—Mark Briggs, David Gray, Thomas Harland, Lawrence Kerwin, William Little, Daniel McGuire, Henry Patton, Lewis Penwright, and Albert Sanderson.

†July 14, 1917.

tall old Highlander, big-boned and grizzled, with a nose like a blue carrot, came in to close the ports.

"Pfat you boys been up to?" he asked. "Desertin' or pfat?"

We told him. The sympathy dropped from his voice.

"No good at all," he said. "They'll mek you when you get to the other side."

The weather grew worse. The *Waitemata* gave us, and no doubt everyone else, but particularly us because we were right over the screw, a very rough time. She pitched and rolled and writhed and groaned. The rudder chains, which ran open along the deck, thumped and rattled and banged just over our heads, and ultimately broke, being replaced by rope. She shipped seas continually and the water spurted through her deck planks. She was aged, decrepit, and hardly seaworthy, but she carried her full complement of troops, including a detachment of measles convalescents, not yet out of quarantine, dumped on board from camp "to make up the quota."

Most of us were sick for the first few days, and though after that we were no longer actively sick, I, for one, felt squeamish throughout the voyage. There were no utensils of any kind in the cabin, and we had to ask permission every time we wished to go to the latrines and be taken up on deck by a guard, the latrines consisting of a rail running along the side of the ship. On one of my first expeditions up there I put my hand on the bulwark, wishing to have a look at the sea. The guard seized me from behind: "No, don't you try going over there," and he did not seem satisfied with my explanation.

We could not help being sick, and as a result the place— stuffy and ill-ventilated as it was with the portholes shut and fourteen men constantly in it—stank. It was enough to upset the stoutest stomach. Briggs and one other man alone stuck it out, but in the end I believe even they succumbed, for a short time at least. By the third day we were equal to argument again. Only Kirwan still lay, silent in his bunk. He was soon afterwards removed to hospital, suffering from some form of kidney trouble, and on the voyage we saw him no more. We were told, however, that he had taken it on. Quite untrue, but it was a method that was often tried.

We had steamed east when we left Wellington, making for South America. When we had been out a few days we saw land, and it was not long before we recognized Wellington Heads. This puzzled us until we realized that we were passing through Cook Strait, making for the Tasman. This change, of course, must have been due to news of a raider somewhere in the vicinity.

Uniform kits, to the full number of men in the cabin, were pushed in. Some of the men opened them and investigated, remarking that they meant to use the underclothing; they badly needed a change.

"Don't touch them," said Briggs.

I said: "Chuck them all through the porthole."

The majority disapproved of destroying all that good clothing. "I would not think of property in a fight like this," I said. "If we heave it overboard it will show the military where we stand, better than anything else."

I had no scruples about the destruction of military equipment when it was being forced on to me against my will. Why should we care about the value of this stuff when we were resisting a power that was destroying life and property every day and even now sending us all to the trenches? But I was hardly taken seriously.

Briggs said he was certain we had no need to worry. They might take us to England, but, when they found we were still sticking out, they wouldn't dare to touch a hair of our heads and in the end they would have to send us back to New Zealand.

The following day an officer came to the clink and

ordered us to put on the uniforms. We all refused. Thereupon we were taken one by one up the stairs to the poop deck. Some resisted and were carried up. I was one of those who walked. We were taken out on the hatchway, and, in front of the crowds of men assembled to watch, stripped naked one by one and forcibly dressed in uniform. The first man to be stripped called out as he stood naked on the deck: "Is there no one man enough to shoot me!"

I was almost the last and had the opportunity to observe the proceedings as a spectator until near the end. The feeling of the watching crowd appeared to be mixed. There was some laughter, some jeering, and a gramophone somewhere played "Onward, Christian Soldiers," but there were also shouts of "Stick it out! Stick to your principles!" The hands of the man who put the uniform on me were trembling so violently that he could hardly carry out his job.

"Don't blame us," he murmured. "Don't blame us. We don't want to do it. We have to."

Back in the clink we started to take the uniform off. An officer standing in the doorway called out: "Bring ropes and tie them up!"

Briggs, nearest the door, called back: "Yes, tie me up! Put me in the darkest dungeon on the boat and I'll be just the same!"

We waited for a while for the threat to be carried out, but nothing happened, and, after a time, our own clothes were returned to us and we put them on. On the same day each one of us was taken up on deck to have his hair cropped to the skin. We all went without resistance except Briggs who was dragged up the stairs and dragged down again after the operation. We could hear his heels rattling and bumping on the stairs first going up, then coming down. The door was opened and he was fired head first in amongst us. He picked himself up, and after he had cooled down a little, he gave us an account of what had happened. He had been held down by six men, but in spite of that he had managed to jerk his head about while the hair-cutting was in progress, with the result that his cropped head was covered with red marks.

We were all somewhat shaken by our ordeal. It was not possible to go through such an experience unscathed. We had to collect our forces again and face an altered situation. They were evidently prepared to go to greater lengths against us than most of us had thought, in those early days before we fully realized what we were up against. Briggs refused to be daunted. Knowing what had been done with the English objectors,* he still believed that the worst that awaited us was imprisonment in England. We had only to continue to stand firm and they would realize the hopelessness of trying to compel us to wear uniform. They had already admitted it by giving us back our own clothes. I did not agree with him. It was my belief that if we were got back to New Zealand it would be in uniform. Did I think they were all going to give in? Briggs asked.

"No, but I think we'll all land back in uniform. Are you prepared to go naked all the time? Because that's what it will mean. Our own clothes won't last for ever; even if they do return them to us every time, which is not likely, I mean to stand out as long as I can on the uniform, but I do see I may not be able to. That doesn't mean giving in."

Briggs' more optimistic outlook had the support of the majority. I think Briggs wanted to keep their spirits up. He told me as much afterwards. Perhaps he was right, though I was inclined to think it was better to be prepared beforehand. We remained shut up in the clink except for short periods of exercise on deck. We called at Albany but saw little of it as we

---

*What they were not aware of was that British conditions were much worse. Of 1,543 objectors imprisoned, 73 died of hardships. These included poor food, overwork, horrendous beatings, and forced feeding of hunger strikers; 31 went insane.

were shut up below must of the time. Magazines—amongst them, to my surprise, a *Ploughshare*—were sent in to us by some padre who took pity on our lack of occupation. We came to know one another and to find out things held in common apart from the bond that united us all—resistance to military service. I found in Sanderson, one of the religious objectors, an interest in literature, particularly in poetry, and many an hour did we spend in the little end cabin, talking over questions far removed from war or our fight against it. His was a gentle, kindly nature, too fine and sensitive to become hardened to the harsh and cruel experience through which he was being made to pass. His religion as he expounded it—he was a Russellite*—was a religion of love; war and violence being negations of love, were impossible to him and against the tenets of his religion. It was also against its tenets to plead in court, and he had refused to speak at his court-martial, being for this reason adjudged defiant and sentenced to six months hard labor. He had served a few weeks of this at the Terrace jail, being probably considered not strong enough for the work at Mt. Cook, for his health was not of the best. Those few weeks had been very hard on him. The atmosphere of repression, the mental degradation, and the physical hardships had depressed him and greatly lowered his vitality.

The little end cabin was considered the special preserve of the seniors. Jack had taken it for himself, but during the day he had to share it with any of us who wished to talk there. I often had long talks with Briggs in there, sitting beside the ventilator shaft. Down it often hurtled packets of cigarettes, chocolate, and fruit, which proved to us that we were not entirely without sympathizers amongst the troops. For food we had what the rest of the men got: passable, nothing wonderful, but certainly no punishment diet. One day, steak of

---

*A follower of the philosopher Bertrand Russell.

the very best, beautifully cooked, was sent in to us. We afterwards heard the cook getting into trouble over it.

"They're men after my own heart," he shouted, "and they should have the best!"

The younger men amused themselves in their own way, played about and wrestled, held mock trials, and made up ridiculous limericks. I joined in, to the scandal of Briggs, who thought us all very undignified and who constantly recalled us to the fact that we had a standard to keep up.

Cases of measles began to appear in the isolation ward, the infection having been spread by the convalescents put on board at Wellington. As the only access to the clink was through the ward, it was almost inevitable that those of us who had not had measles should contract them. Sandy was the first. A few days later I followed, and then Jack and Sanderson. Sandy was only a mild case and was up by the time we were at our worst. Most of the cases were pretty bad. Measles, from a camp infection, can be bad. I had been in the ward a day or two when it was evidently discovered that the sentence of twenty-eight days detention given me in Trentham had run out. An officer came to my bedside. A uniform was brought, and, nervously and awkwardly, he asked me if I would accept it if I were well enough to put it on. My temperature was high and I was feeling light-headed, but I realized what was going on. I said: "No." It was then formally offered to me; I refused it, and was forthwith sentenced to twenty-eight days detention. The orderlies were anxious to do their best, but they were untrained and there was only one doctor on the ship. Some of the orderlies saw nothing amiss in a temperature of 112 degrees caused by washing the thermometer in hot water. When my temperature was at its highest and I was feeling like nothing on earth, one of them came up to my bed with a heaped plateful of fried fish and potatoes.

"This will do you good," he said, smiling hopefully.

He was very disappointed when he found I couldn't touch it. Sandy thought he would do better. He brought me some tinned fruit he had somehow obtained. It looked very inviting, but when I came to try it, I couldn't touch it, either. The uneasy motion of the *Waitemata*, keeping us continually moving, made things much worse, and the finishing touch was the unfitness of the ward to house sickness at any time. The *Waitemata* shipped seas continually, even in comparatively calm weather, and the water pushed aside the tarpaulin over the hatchway, and found its way into the ward, pouring water over the beds directly beneath. One unfortunate man received the full force of the water on his bed. He died shortly afterwards, whether in consequence or not, I don't know.

One night there was great excitement. Lights could be seen. By morning we were at the wharf at Capetown. A strange doctor, evidently the Port Health Officer, came into the ward. He went round the beds, looking stern and angry and giving sharp orders. Behind him came the troopship's one doctor and some of the other officers. He pointed to beds.

"I'll have that one and that one," until he had nearly all the cases in the ward. "Have them on the wharf in half an hour."

Two orderlies came round to my bedside with a stretcher.

"No," I said, not liking the thought of being carried. "I think I'll manage."

I dressed, and though feeling pretty shaky, got up on deck and down the gangway to the wharf. No chance of saying good-bye to the others. Jack had come off the boat with me and Sanderson. We afterwards heard that the *Waitemata* was condemned by the South African authorities as unfit for the transport of troops, and all the men on her were transferred to boats of the Union Castle Line.

4

WE SAT, or lay, as the case might be, on the wharf and waited. A chill wind blew in from the bay and in our weakened condition, only just risen from bed, we felt it keenly. It seemed a very long time before lorries drove on to the wharf and we were loaded on to them, stretcher cases and walking cases indiscriminately. Though I knew that Jack and Sanderson had come off with me, I could not see them afterwards on the wharf and they were not put on the same lorry with me.

We turned off the wharf and ran up through the town to the Maitland Hospital, on high ground in view of Table Mountain. Here we were unloaded on to a level space of grass. Nothing was ready, no tents up. We had to wait about until at last the tents were erected in the long, wet grass and beds brought in. Then, thankfully, we all went to bed again, in sheets and pajamas and all manner of things to which we had long been unaccustomed. Only one lorry had come up; the others had gone elsewhere, and in them Jack and Sanderson. I suppose we had to be distributed wherever accommodation was to be found.

It was pleasant in the tent when once we were comfortably settled in bed. Bright-faced, smiling black "boys" brought us in our food and ministered to our wants, and nurses came in to us from the main hospital. Most of the men recovered quickly under the improved conditions, fresh air, and attention. One man, however, who had been unconscious for some time before we left the boat, rose suddenly in bed when there happened to be no nurses in the tent, got up, and made for the tent door. Before we could realize what had happened, or do anything, he had fallen over the tent ropes. When we asked how he was a little later, we were told that he was dead. The nurses came round asking us all for information about him. His people had to be written to, and it was hard to find anything to say. Finally, something was got together and sent off.

The matron, middle-aged and ginger-haired, came on her rounds in the morning and usually brought oranges to the patients.

"Catch, conscientious objector," she would say to me with a grin and throw an orange to me.

She accompanied the different doctors on their visits to us. One of them came in with her.

"Baxter is a conscientious objector," she told him when they came to my bed.

"How do you come to be here?" he asked and I told him, briefly.

"You're far too good a Highlander, Baxter," he said, "not to be fighting for your king. When you get to France you'll be throwing Germans over your head on your bayonet."

"Yes, my ancestors fought for the king, except when they happened to be fighting against him. I'm fighting, too, only I'm on a different tack. I'm fighting against a war."

"Oh, well," he said, "they might get you a job rocking cradles."

"If people of your views run the world," I answered, "there soon won't be any cradles to rock."

The matron squeaked and jumped back. The men looked

as if they expected something dreadful to happen and seemed surprised when nothing came of it.

The next doctor was of a different type. The matron introduced me in the usual way.

"The first conscientious objector I've ever had, doctor. I've never seen one before."

"No, we haven't got conscription here," he said. "If we had you'd see plenty."

He turned to me. "I think a man has a perfect right to his own mind: I don't blame any man for standing to his principles. You certainly have courage or you wouldn't be standing out the way you are."

I came to know the other men who were with me. At first, before we were well enough to talk much or get about, they were inclined to regard me as the men in the clink were regarded by most of the troops on the transport, as a man of anti-social outlook, incapable of mixing with other men. On the *Waitemata* they had had no opportunity of altering this view, as they did not come into contact with us. At the hospital it was a different matter. I think that view of me was finally dispelled when they returned one day from a walk and found me playing draughts* with another man who had remained behind. We could not take long walks as we had to keep within bounds, but we could wander some distance in the neighborhood of the hospital.

I have little but pleasant recollections of South Africa. It was a strange interlude—a respite—in a strenuous fight. I had never seen any land but my own and this was absolutely different from it. The light, buoyant air, the strange smell that seemed to pervade everything, the vivid coloring of the shrubs and flowers, made it a new world for me. Even the queer South African sheep, hardly like sheep at all, with their enormous tails, sometimes weighing as much as fifteen

*Checkers.

pounds, and the exceedingly tough mutton they made, was a novelty. At night, from the lagoon which lay below the hospital, there floated up through the clear air a sound like myriad tiny bells. In the rest of the world frogs croak, but not here. The same rosy cloud lies over a visit I paid to a dentist, just at the close of my stay in hospital. Never have I known such gentleness and such skill.

Our sojourn in that place of pleasant convalescence had to come to an end. When we were considered to be safely out of quarantine, we were all collected up and taken to the Castle. It was a large building of brick and stone, dating from the time of the Dutch occupation. It had outer walls immensely thick and high, with flat tops from which a wide view of the town could be obtained. Inside there were yards and further walls, making part of the main building.

I was taken to the guardroom, which was just inside the outer gate. Part of the room was barred off like a cage at the Zoo. Behind the bars men were sitting, standing, and lying about, some still drunk, others recovering. I could see Jack in amongst them, looking disheveled and dirty. It was a horrible place. So many bodies crowded together exhaled a fetid smell.

The sergeant who had brought us in from the hospital said to me: "Sorry to say I'll have to put you in here."

"Put me in there!" I said. "You'll do nothing of the kind! You have no authority to shut me up!"

"Haven't I? We'll soon see."

"Take me before the officer in charge here," I said, and much against his will he did so.

The officer was a lieutenant in the South African forces, New Zealand born. I explained my position; that I had resisted military service in New Zealand and had been deported, still resisting; that the sentence I had been given on the boat had run out and that I had not been charged with a fresh offense. I also said that my brother was down below in the guardroom and that his position was the same as my own. He sent for Jack and went through our papers, which he had beside him. From them he soon verified the facts.

"It's twenty years since I was in New Zealand," he said, "and I don't know what laws they have there now. I hear they have conscription, but it seems strange to me that, even under conscription, they should send men out of New Zealand in civil clothes. However, I've got nothing to do with that. We haven't got conscription here, anyway, and while you're here I won't give you any orders or require you to do anything. All I ask of you is not to attempt to escape."

I assured him that we had not the slightest intention of escaping.

"And I would like you to answer the roll," he said. "It makes it easier for us."

We agreed to do so.

Jack told me that he was thankful to get out. The place was crawling, he said. But we did not escape vermin. Nearly everyone in the Castle was lousy, and it was very hard, in fact impossible, to get rid of them. No sooner did one manage to, than one acquired them again from others.

Jack told me that Sanderson had been sent to the military prison at Wynberg, after he came out of quarantine, to serve the rest of his sentence he had received in New Zealand. It seemed very hard that Sanderson, of all of us the least fit to stand it, should spend his time in South Africa shut up in a cell, deprived of all chance of seeing the strange new country, which would have interested him so much, and of the freedom which would have given him a chance to make a proper recovery.

A Home Officer came to the Castle and harangued the troops on the color question.

"You men are accustomed to a different attitude on the matter of color in New Zealand. I've heard that you look on your Maoris as social equals. But I want you to understand that here, in South Africa, for a man to be on friendly terms with a colored person, or even to be seen talking with one in a social way, is a crime. I believe that some of you have been seen in the town in the company of colored people and I want you to understand how that is looked on here."

The attitude of a lifetime is not altered in one day. The New Zealanders are freer from the color complex than almost any race on earth. They saw no reason why they should not be on friendly terms with an amiable and harmless people and took very little notice of the warning, and continued to mix with them. Probably as a consequence of this, all leave was stopped for the ranks, and they were confined within the Castle walls.

We had often argued with the nurses at the hospital over the same thing. We asked them for the reason for the attitude of the whites in Cape Colony towards the colored population. They could give us no clear reason. They just knew the blacks had to be kept under or they would be dangerous.

"But what about these Negroes that help in the hospital?" we asked.

"Oh, that's different," said the nurses. "Those are our boys. They're specially chosen and we know they're all right." At the same time we could see that they looked upon those "boys" not as ordinary human beings but as a sort of special pet dog, to whom one should be kind. Almost every day I saw in the papers reports of sentences of flogging imposed on natives. One day, I remember, there were seventeen cases of natives charged with some such offense as being found in the garden of a European; and in fifteen of them sentences of flogging were imposed. Most of the offenses were merely minor ones, for which a fine, or at most a few days imprisonment, would have been imposed in New Zealand. South Africans say, of course, that we don't understand their problems, and that if we did we would know that that is the only way to deal with the natives. I can't believe that it will prove the right way in the long run.

Confinement to the Castle was very irksome with Capetown lying invitingly below us and any amount of exploring to be done. But we were not allowed out on any pretext. There was only one gate in the outer wall and that was guarded. The walls were extremely high and impossible to scale. It was generally agreed that escape was impossible.

Jack and I were one day walking on the flat top of the inner walls, discussing the question of escape.

"I know how I could get out," said Jack, "but the trouble is, I couldn't get you out, too."

"I'll manage that for myself," I said. "I'm going out now. You stay up here and when you see me appear in the street, you put your scheme into operation and follow me. I'll wait for you down there."

I went down to the temporary huts in the yard, where we all messed and slept: "Any of you chaps want anything in town? Because I'm going out."

They refused to take me seriously, but at least one Irishman said he wanted a tin of tobacco and gave me the money. I went into the inner yard. From the officers' quarters on the opposite side came three officers. I looked through the archway to the outer yard and the gate. The sentry had not seen me. I fell in behind the officers. As they neared the gate I drew abreast of them. We all passed through the gate, the guard looking suspiciously at me but deciding that I must be known to the officers, and the officers looking questioningly at the guard but deciding I must be known to him as he was not challenging me. I kept an absolutely unmoved face. Once outside and out of sight of the guard, I dropped behind, crossed over the street, and signaled to Jack, far back on the wall. I waited. I waited half an hour and he did not appear. It was growing late, so I made the circuit of the Castle walls and went down into the town. I bought the tobacco and hurried back, the problem of breaking in again weighing on my mind. There was a light burning over the archway and the gate was shut. I drew to the side and waited for something to turn up. A few minutes later a car drove up and turned in at the gate. I ran in behind it and it passed me. In this way I got through the gate, but the guard saw me.

"Halt!" he called and rushed at me with the bayonet. "It's the guardroom for you."

"Right," I said and waited, thankful I had been caught breaking in and not breaking out. The guard went over to shut the gate and got out his keys. I had been edging round the angle of the wall, and when I saw him occupied with the lock of the gate, I made a dash for it and got safely through the archway in the inner wall. I might have got a bullet in the back, but I did not think it likely he would fire and I knew he would not pursue me or, for his own sake, say anything about it afterwards. He saw me the next day when he was off duty, but he only grinned. I came into the hut with the tobacco. They were all immensely impressed.

"You must have squared the guards," they said.

"I give you my word I didn't. You know I have no money."

They pressed me to tell my method, but I wouldn't. I asked Jack why he had not followed me, and he said he couldn't be sure it was me signaling, it was so far away and the light was bad.

We made tours of inspection all over the Castle, wherever we were allowed to go, and that was almost everywhere. We found the execution yard, a sinister square surrounded by high walls. There was a place in one wall where victims had been buried.

In one of the cells of the Castle a German was confined, charged with causing a riot in a tea shop. According to what we were told he had quarreled with a man over the war and fought with him. I could hardly see that this constituted a riot or that he had committed a very serious crime. He was said to be very violent and he certainly looked it when we saw him exercising in the corridor, always in handcuffs. But handcuffs in themselves are inclined to make a man look violent, and I have sometimes wondered, in the light of my own experience later on, whether he really was. We used to see him eating his meals with his hands freed for the purpose and he never made any attempt to attack the guard at these times. Defiant he certainly was and we could not but admire his pluck. Quite alone, surrounded by enemies, and entirely in their power, he never failed to hold his head high and to hurl defiance at them whenever he had the opportunity. "Never" is perhaps incorrect, because in one instance he did, for a moment, quail. His court-martial had been behind closed doors, but his sentence was promulgated in public. When he heard it—ten years penal servitude—he dropped his head and flinched as from a blow. From the walls we could see the civil prison, where he was probably sent. The prisoners were all in white. The distance was too great for us to distinguish the Europeans from the natives; they all looked the same in that white uniform. They appeared to do everything at the double and never to move at a walk.

The troops in the huts were made up of measles cases from the *Waitemata*, men from former drafts who had missed their boats, and men on their way back from France, both Australians and New Zealanders. On the whole they were a fairly peaceable lot, apart from spasmodic personal quarrels. But when payday came, beer being obtainable within the walls and there being no other way of spending the money, things became pretty hot for a while. It was only natural, given a body of men shut up in a restricted area with nothing to do and unlimited access to beer. Fights were frequent at these times. One man came within an ace of having his throat cut and only saved himself by holding his chin down and getting it split instead. When the last effects of the drink had cleared away the combatants were perfectly friendly again.

A considerable amount of damage was done during these periodic outbreaks. Crockery and furniture were smashed and jam tins would come hurtling through the windows at the heads of the Dutch guards outside. Finally, the South African authorities got tired of it and sent us all off to Simonstown, some miles down the coast towards the Cape. The change was greatly for the better. Here we could go where we pleased as long as we returned to camp before a certain hour.

Simonstown lay on the spit of land running down the coast from Capetown and ending up in the Cape of Good Hope. It was located on the inside of the spit, looking over the wide bay (called False Bay in the atlases, but I always heard it called Simons Bay). Large ships could come almost to the shore, the water deepening immediately from the land. In the evening, a long line of fishing boats would come in from the open sea under sail. The surrounding country was wonderful, different from anything we had ever known. A plateau rose at the back of the town, running up into high granite peaks. Beyond, the bay hills rose into the haze and to the north further plateaus were crowned by high hills. At the top of one of the hills, which we used often to climb, we found an old Dutch cemetery, overgrown with trees and shrubs. The gravestones were fallen and lying in all directions and a peaceful melancholy lay over it all.

I used to go down to the shore and watch the natives fishing. Numbers would gather up and go out in boats. Their course was often directed by an old gray-haired Negro, who would stand on a rock above the beach and signal to them which direction to take. His knowledge of the whereabouts of fish was uncanny. He would direct them which way to pull the nets and sometimes he would signal: "No good. Come in."

The natives all believed he could see the fish in the water. Of one thing there is no doubt. He knew where the fish were, for I watched often and he made no mistakes. When he said, "They've lost them," the nets would come in empty, and when he said, "They've got them," they would come in with shoals of fish. All the natives showed great respect for the old man. Some of the Negro boys fished from the shore, and I did, too, and sometimes got quite a good catch.

One day I gave my catch to a boy who had not been successful and he took them home with him. Next day he turned up with a dozen eggs for me, saying his mother had sent them. Afterwards I questioned him about his life and his family. He told me his father and mother were Christians, that they thought war and violence wrong and contrary to the teaching of Christ.

As the spring advanced, new varieties of flowers and shrubs came out almost every day. The brilliance of their coloring was almost tropical. Scarlet predominated, but there was purple, yellow, and pink as well. Round the base of the mountains for miles grew a belt of scarlet and purple gladioli, and on the mountains themselves gray varieties of the white and pink everlasting daisy as large as saucers. I used to go far afield and return with bunches of flowers that were rare in the neighborhood of town. From the sale of these flowers I got all the money we needed while we were there. They were usually ordered beforehand and people would give 2s. 6d. for a small bunch. Of course, it took a lot of hunting to get them, but it was pleasant work in which my brother joined heartily and the money came in very handy at the time.

We went on expeditions with the other men, exploring and snake-hunting in the hills. We had little fear of snakes, probably because we knew so little about them. I became quite an expert at curing snake skins and the skins of enormous furry green caterpillars which we found on our walks. Brilliantly colored birds abounded. Up in caves in the hills we found monkeys. The female monkeys would stand at the entrance of caves in the cliffside, quite inaccessible to us, and look down on us in fear and anger, holding their young in their arms. While I was in Simonstown, a monkey who had evidently quarreled with his tribe came down into the town and remained there on perfectly friendly terms with human beings.

Men were constantly passing through Simonstown on their way back from France to New Zealand. One day a new Sergeant-Major came on duty at the camp. He, too, was on his way back from France. He addressed the men. He wanted them, he said, to have some idea of what they were going to, not to land over there, as he had, absolutely ignorant of what awaited them.

"The war's ruined me," he said, "as it's ruined many a better man. I hope you're going to have a better time than I had. I hope you won't have to go through the things that I went through. Perhaps the war will be over by the time you get there, though it doesn't look much like it. The things I've seen and done I can't get out of my mind. Cold-blooded killing of defenseless men. I've got a wife and three little boys: you'd think I'd be glad to be going back to them, but I'm not. I feel I can't face them with these things on my mind, and here's the New Zealand government brought in conscription and forcing men into that hell. Sending them over in civilian clothes like these two here."

The men were astonished at hearing such things from the lips of a Sergeant-Major, but they were curious, and crowded round him asking questions.

"Once," he said, "we took a lot of German prisoners. About seventy, there were. Then we got orders that we weren't to take any prisoners. So we stood them up against a bank and killed them all in cold blood—bayoneted them. I know other nations do the same. I know the Germans do. It's just war, and war is hell, and the men who make it, bloody bastards."

Next day there was another Sergeant-Major in his place.

Spring gave place to summer and the best of the flowers were over. Everything was getting dried up and it was becoming very hot before we entrained for Capetown, towards the end of November. There were a number of women at the station at Capetown when we arrived, presenting all the soldiers with ditty bags. I was given one too. I didn't like to refuse it in case I hurt the feelings of the donor. Seeing me with the others, though I was in civil clothes, she would look on me as one of the rest.

When we came on board the *Llanstephan Castle,* we found Sanderson. Shut up in a cell all the time while we had had our freedom, he had not recovered from the effects of measles as we had, and was looking more depressed than I had ever seen him. He had not been badly treated on the whole, he said. They had told him at the prison that it was not their business to compel him to work, and they had not done so, but they had kept him shut up most of the time.

The officer in charge of the troops on board, an Australian, said to me: "I have nothing to do with what the New Zealand government is trying with you men, and I don't intend to interfere with you in any way or to give you any orders. I only make one request of you; that is, to take part in lifeboat drill. It's a necessary precaution for the safety of everyone and has nothing to do with the army."

For my part I felt that this was perfectly reasonable, and the other two agreed with me in acceding to his request.

We were on very friendly terms with all the New Zealanders. We mixed with them without any restriction and made the voyage under very different conditions from those on the trip to South Africa. One of the New Zealanders came to me and pressed a sum of money onto me.

"We've made it up amongst us," he said. "We know you have no money and we don't like to see it, so we want you to take this."

"I couldn't think of taking it," I said. "It's very good of you, and I do appreciate it, but I don't like to think of men being asked to give when they have little enough themselves."

No one had been asked to give, he said. All those who had given had been keen to. So I wasn't to worry about that, and they wouldn't like it at all if I didn't accept.

In the end I did, as I saw my refusal would offend them. Jack and Sanderson were very touched at this token of sympathy and quite agreed that it was not possible to refuse it.

Early in the voyage Sanderson went down with dysentery. In poor health, as he already was, he seemed to have no resistance. He was very ill—so ill that for a time I thought he would never reach England. However, he pulled round and was about again by the time we arrived at Plymouth.

There were nine hundred Negroes on board. They were clad in an ugly dark chocolate uniform which was extremely unbecoming to their complexions. They were not at all pleased with it themselves and looked longingly on the khaki. One of the New Zealanders on board, nicknamed for some reason Harry Lauder, seeing an opportunity for money-making in this desire of the Negroes, sold them as many khaki uniforms as he could lay hands on from the stores. Numbers of Negroes blossomed out in them. There was a great uproar. Being questioned, they said they had bought them from a man at two shillings apiece. Asked if they could point out the man, they said they could. Brought up on deck, they immediately identified Harry Lauder. He had managed to secrete the money somewhere so that it was never discovered, and the Negroes were the losers, having to give up the uniforms without getting their money back.

We touched at St. Helena, but no one was allowed to go ashore. Some of the inhabitants came on board and we got some information from them about the kind of life they led on the island. From the ship it looked to us to be only a bare rock, its cliffs rising up sheer from the deep ocean. I was surprised to hear that about three thousand people were living there, engaged in hemp cultivation. We could see no sign of their settlement, only rock, but there must have been some land further back on top. We saw the high rock where Napoleon used to stand alone, gazing at the sea. As a boy, I had had considerable admiration for him. I wondered what his thoughts were as he stood there. Was it there he said: "The longer I live the more I am convinced that no lasting system of government can be founded on force?" Napoleon professed to believe in peace and his goal was the United States of Europe. His method was force—and force had crushed him at last—and yet that force could not give Europe peace.

We sailed away from St. Helena and our next call was Sierra Leone. We lay out at some distance from the shore, and the natives came out in their wonderful tree-trunk canoes, which were hollowed in a single piece out of the trunk, and yet were only a shell and as light as a feather. They brought out fruit and things to sell, and dived for coins, though there were sharks in other parts of the bay. We stayed for a day or two, and each morning a red fiery sun climbed up the sky until the atmosphere was like the breath of a furnace. The glow of the sunset on the trees and buildings on shore was unlike anything I had ever seen. I can never forget the morning we sailed away. The sea was as still as a mill-pond, except where great sharks circled about, their huge fins projecting above the water. Beautiful little islets with stately palm trees and red-roofed houses were mirrored in the clear water. From these there floated out to us as it were the music of many flutes.

5

WE ARRIVED AT Plymouth the day after Christmas, 1917. So short a time ago we had sailed out of a tropic harbor and here the land was covered with snow, woods, and hamlets showing up black against the expanse of white. As we disembarked an English officer, standing on the wharf, asked who the men in civil clothes were. He was told.

"Conscientious objectors! What on earth does New Zealand mean, sending conscientious objectors here? As if we hadn't enough to do with our own!"

We traveled from Plymouth to the Salisbury Plain by railway. We passed through beautiful hilly country all smoothed to uniformity under its mantle of snow. Finally we came to Sling, lying out on the Plain.

The day after our arrival we were all medically examined and it was found that many of the men who had been in the Castle at Capetown, amongst them Jack and myself, were suffering from scabies. Those who had had measles seemed to have been particularly susceptible to it. We were isolated and underwent several days treatment, which consisted of submersion of everything except the face in sulfur baths almost hotter than one could stand. After the treatment was over, we rejoined Sanderson, whose imprisonment at Wynberg had saved him from lice.

For a day or two we were at liberty about the camp. Someone told me that a mate of mine was over at one of the huts. I was very anxious to find out something about the rest of the fourteen and hurrying over I found Gray stooping over a fire, heating something in an oil drum. He explained his being in uniform. The authorities, he said, had wanted him to wear it while they communicated with New Zealand and found out what to do about him. His case was quite different from the others, they told him. He was regarded as genuine and would probably be sent back to New Zealand. He had taken it on and had been doing a little gardening about the camp, expecting at any time to hear that he was being sent back. But time had passed and he had heard nothing. He was wondering now if it had not all been a scheme to get him to take service in the army. I asked him if he knew what had happened to the others. They had all been sent over to France, he said, about two months ago. What had happened to them there he did not know, but he had heard all sorts of rumors.

"They say," he said, "that you and Briggs will be shot."

They had had a pretty rough time coming over from South Africa in the *Norman Castle*, he told me. They were forcibly dressed in uniform, their own clothes taken away and not returned to them. When they took the uniform off and went about in underclothes, the underclothes were taken away. They were hosed down and then dressed only in uniform. Though they had been brought out on deck in front of the passengers, they took the uniform off and went naked. After a while they managed to get underclothes again and went about in them. Before landing they were dressed in uniform again and some of them who refused to walk were dragged off. We had certainly missed hardships through having measles.

The following day, Jack, Sanderson, and I were taken before the officer in command at Sling. There was none of the usual military formality about the interview. No escort tramping in with shouts of "Stand to attention." It was like an interview with a businessman or a lawyer. We were given chairs. The absence of formality and restraint made it much easier for us to express ourselves.

He began by saying: "I have heard of you men before, but I have never met any of you. I am very much interested and I want to hear your side of the case, what your standpoint is, and how you have acted up 'til now. I believe you have had a pretty bad time."

I said I would speak for myself and my brother, who could correct me if he wished. Sanderson could speak for himself. I gave an account of our experiences in New Zealand, on the *Waitemata*, and in South Africa. He listened and asked questions, showing no hostility, and during the whole interview was pleasant and sympathetic. He asked me if I were patriotic, in the sense of caring for my country and wishing its welfare.

I said I did care for my country and that to my mind there was nothing more necessary for the welfare of a country than to keep from going to war. "Whatever wars were in the past," I said, "we have come to the point in civilization now when war can do nothing but harm to every nation that engages in it. But in peacetime a nation must so live and act toward other nations as not to provoke war. We must be prepared to make sacrifices, but they will be nothing like the sacrifices a nation has to make in war, to gain nothing by them but the prospect of further wars." He asked: "Do you think a mere handful of men, standing for an ideal, is going to have any effect?"

I said that we did hope to have an effect, that there were

men in other countries making the same stand, "and as for being only a handful in standing for a cause, someone has to begin if the cause is ever to be won. I think, too, that there are people who look on war as we do."

"I know there are thousands who look on war as you do, but they don't take your stand."

"We hope by our action to make some of those people, at any rate, to stand to their convictions, and only by bringing people to our point of view and getting them to stand to their convictions shall we ever achieve our ideal."

He asked: "Do you look upon the things that are happening to you, and will happen to you, just as a misfortune, or do you feel that in suffering them you are serving your ideal?"

"Of course, in this I can only speak for myself, but I do feel that I am fighting for a warless world where peoples can live together in peace and friendship, as most of them really want, though they can be roused to hatred and violence."

"You realize, of course, that you will not have an easy time. How far are you prepared to go?"

"To answer honestly, I am prepared to stand to the utmost limit."

"Are you open to conviction?" he asked.

I said I was, but I had not yet heard any arguments that would have any hope of convincing me.

"If you knew that your action would have no effect, would you still go on?"

I said that my individual action would be the same, though in that case I would not have the hope I had now. Jack said he was entirely in agreement with what I had said.

Sanderson then stated his case. He said his attitude was based on the tenets of the religious sect to which he belonged. They held that all wars, force, and violence were wrong and opposed to the teaching of Christ. His was a religion of love. People, when told about it, often said it was too good to be true, but if everyone followed it, all strife and trouble would vanish from the world. He was standing for what he believed to be right and would continue to stand for it as far as he could. Asked if he were open to conviction, he said he was, but he was sure that no one would ever convince him.

At the close of the interview, which seemed to have lasted all morning, the officer said: "I am very glad to have met you and to have got all this information. I want to tell you that you have convinced me beyond question of your courage and sincerity. Now, I shall probably not see you again, for I shall not be here after tomorrow, and you will be in other hands. I have not entered into argument with you because I feel I don't know enough about the subject, whereas you have gone into it very thoroughly. I don't wish to advise you in any way as to what you should do, but I wish you well."

We went back to our usual quarters with the men who had come with us from Capetown. Sanderson, however, was separated from us. The next day we were told he had taken it on. I thought it very unlikely after the strong case he had put up the previous day. But it was true. The next time I saw him he was in uniform. He told me that when he found out what methods they were going to use against him, he realized that he would not be able to hold out.

"I don't think much of them," he said. "The nation that can bring itself to use such methods against us has sunk pretty low."

I didn't think much of them either. They had forced a man—one of the finest characters I had ever met, weakened by ill-health and ill-treatment—to act against his strongly held convictions. A victory, if they liked to call it one.

We were soon removed from our quarters with the other men and put into one of the regimental guardrooms. We were not, however, under close arrest, but had the freedom of the guardroom and the yard belonging to it. Every day we were taken before Colonel Howard. He looked worn and ill to me, but that may only have been his natural appearance. In my mind it excused his manner to us. From the start he was stern and hostile. He said he knew all about us and what sort of time we had had. We were now at the finish and it would be either one thing or the other. However, we were to be given one more chance to think over taking it on. I said there was no need for me to think it over. I was taking on nothing in the army. Jack, however, said he would think it over, and we were returned to the guardroom. The next day, hearing we were still of the same mind, the Colonel said: "I want you to understand that this is your only chance of taking on some form of non-combatant service. I don't say it will be offered to you. I don't say that you will get it. But if you don't agree to take on something of the sort, you will be sent straight to the trenches. Now this is not a threat, it's a fact; you may be sent anyway, but what I am telling you is your only hope. Think it over."

So far, Jack and I had always been together at night, though we had sometimes been separated during the day. The reason given for allowing us to be together at night was that we might discuss the matter.

At my final interview with Howard I was alone. I told him I could only say again what I had already said many times: that I would not take any kind of service in the army.

He said: "You have said what *you* intend to do. Now I will tell you what *we* intend to do. We'll make your life a hell, Baxter."

I told him that it was not in the power of the military to do that; that they could make me suffer, but they couldn't make my life a hell. That lay with me.

"Well, you'll find," he said, "that from now on you'll be compelled to obey."

I was not long back in the guardroom when an escort marched in and removed me to another clink. I did not see

Jack again. On the way over, the guards remarked: "The game's up for you. You're being taken to Sergeant Falk."

"Oh, and what's he like?"

"Wait 'til you see him and you'll soon know."

I was brought into the passage that ran in front of the cells. A uniform lay in readiness. The sergeant in charge of the clink came in, a tall, heavily built man.

"Strip him and put the uniform on him," he ordered. When this had been done he seized me by the shoulders and swung me round against the wall.

"Now you see this," he said, clenching his fist and drawing his arm back, ready to strike. "If you attempt to take the uniform off you'll get this straight in the head and you'll get it again and again, 'til I've knocked bloody daylight through you."

I ripped the buttons of the tunic open and pulled it down over my arms, expecting the blow every moment. To my astonishment he swung round suddenly and went out, calling out as he went: "Don't let him take it off."

They put the tunic on me again and shut me in one of the cells. Dinner was brought in to me, but in spite of the fact that I had by this time removed the tunic they made no attempt to put it on me. It seemed to me that I had won on this. Perhaps it was all threats and they did not intend to go any distance in forcing me.

The Adjutant came in. He began the interview with an assumption of breezy confidence.

"So you're Baxter. I've often wanted to meet an objector, but I never have 'til now." (This was not strictly true, but did as an opening.) "You're in my Company and I think we'll get on very well. I hear you have scruples about taking life. Is that it?"

"Yes, I have scruples about taking life, if you put it that way. I am against war. I think it is wrong and I refuse to have anything to do with it, either in combatant service or in any way that would help in carrying it on."

"You object to taking life? Now I can tell you something about that. What did you have for dinner?"

"I really couldn't put a name to it. Some kind of hash or other."

"Do you mean to say you don't know what you had for dinner? Sergeant, what did this man have for dinner?"

"Well, sir, I couldn't exactly say. It was what was going here, some kind of mixture of biscuits and stuff."

"Did it have meat in it?"

"Why, yes, sir, it had some bits of meat in it."

"That's what I wanted to know. Now," he said, turning to me, "you eat meat. To provide that meat an animal had to die. Now, I have been over in France and I know what's going on there and I can tell you that those Boches who come down on our men in the trenches are no better than animals. In fact, they're a great deal worse than lions and tigahs. So you need have no scruples whatever about killing them."

Ill-suppressed laughter came from the guardroom, where they were all listening.

"Do you mean to say," I exclaimed, "that you expect to influence me by such absolutely ridiculous arguments! All this absurd talk about lions and tigers. You can't tell me that the Germans, a civilized nation like others, are simply wild beasts, while the nations opposed to them remain civilized. I know that when men fight, animal instincts are roused on both sides, but that's war and that's what I am out against."

He dropped his appearance of amiability and became frankly angry.

"Put this man in handcuffs," he ordered, "and keep them on until he promises to obey. And you'll have this off," he said, seizing me by the hair. "I daresay you're very proud of it. See that he gets a haircut, Sergeant."

I did not see that he strengthened his case by being personally offensive. I did still try to keep my hair combed and myself otherwise in order, but that was no reason for attacking me.

The uniform was put on me again. Falk brought a pair of handcuffs and fastened my hands behind my back. A hat was jammed roughly down on my head and I was taken out to get a haircut. I was given a close crop, my hair being cut to the skin. Back in the guardroom, the handcuffs were taken off and I was allowed out in the passage in front of the cells.

I was walking up and down there when the Adjutant appeared the following day, not at all pleased at what he looked on as contravention of his orders.

"What's this man doing out here and not in irons?" he asked, and then to me, "You're having far too easy a time, but you're not going to have it any longer. You won't be allowed out here and you'll be handcuffed the whole time."

Falk protested. "It's so cold in the cells, sir, I don't like putting him in there with the handcuffs on in this weather."

"If he doesn't choose to obey," said the Adjutant, "he can stay in handcuffs 'til he freezes."

The orders were carried out. From that time until the day before I left Sling, three weeks later, the handcuffs were never off except at night while I was in bed and while I took my meals, the guard standing over me ready to put them on again the moment I had taken the last mouthful.

At first I was taken out for exercise every day along the road through the camp on which we were certain to meet the largest number of men both coming and going. The object was, not that I should have the requisite amount of exercise to keep me in health, but that the shame and humiliation of being thus exposed, manacled, to the eyes of the troops, should force me into giving in. I can't say I didn't feel it. I did, intensely, and never ceased to, but it did not have the desired effect.

The military police did not like it at all, and did their best, by walking as close to me as they could, to hide the handcuffs. After a few days of this, they said on coming out of the guard-room: "Let's go round here; it's quiet," and instead of going through the camp, we turned down a road that led immediately into the bare open plain, where we seldom met anyone.

Another day, this time in company with two prisoners from the guardroom, we took a track leading through open fields and along a ridge sparsely covered with a scrubby kind of box, to a wood set high on a hill. On its outer edge was a grove of hazel brush, the bushes as high and strong as trees, with many nuts still on them. My two companions climbed the trees and knocked down the nuts.

One of the guards standing watching said to me: "Now, Baxter, wouldn't you like to do that, too? Give us your word you won't remove the uniform and we'll take the hand-cuffs off."

But that I would not do, and so I had to remain an onlooker. As we came by, the guard who had wanted me to climb the trees remarked: "Well, we've had a pleasant outing, haven't we?"

He spoke, I am sure, only in friendliness, and I replied that I had enjoyed it, but his words were a mockery to me. There was beauty all around us up there on the hill—beauty of bare, leafless trees; of wild blue distance; and open plain. Instead of pleasing me it saddened and hurt me, giving an edge to the contrast between the freedom of nature and my condition, of which the iron shackles were a constant reminder. In the cell I could bear it better, for there was no contrast to cut me. But on the free and open hills the bitter-ness of the struggle was brought home to me in its fullness.

Very soon afterwards these outings ceased, and I got no exercise at all except when I was taken before officers, which meant a walk of only a hundred yards or so. On these occa-sions I was always marched with a great deal of military show on the part of the escort. Shouts of "Halt! Stand to attention!" and my hat would be snatched from my head with a tug that nearly dislocated my jaws, to be jammed on again later, when I would be marched out to the accompaniment of further shouts. The Colonel would ask: "Any charge against this man, Sergeant?"

"No, sir."

As a rule he obviously didn't know what to do with me, asked a few tentative questions, and dismissed me without having arrived anywhere.

It was, as Falk had said, very cold in the cell. When the weather was rough, rain, sleet, and snow came in through the hole high up in the outer wall that ventilated it, and the frost came in when the weather was clear. My blankets were removed during the day and the cell was left absolutely bare. If I wanted to read—and literature was sometimes handed in to the guardroom for me—I had to sit on the floor with the paper beside me and turn my back to it when I had to turn a page. I was often so stiff with the cold and the cramped position of my arms, held always behind me by the handcuffs, that I could hardly move a limb. I developed a violent face ache. No doubt a decayed tooth was the original cause of it, but the cold played its part in intensifying it. The doctor examined my mouth and sent me to the dentist. He looked at my mouth.

"You'd better write his name on the card," he said to one of the orderlies.

"It seems a shame to let his name go in amongst the other men's," said the orderly.

"That's so, but there has to be some record kept." To me he said: "There's a good deal to do. If we fix up your mouth for you, you'll promise to take on service in the army?"

"What's that got to do with you?" I asked. "I never asked to be brought here."

"No, but you said you had toothache."

"You're trying to make a bargain with me over my teeth. I won't promise to do anything at all."

"In that case we can do nothing for you," he said.

I was irritated by the feeling that I had been made a fool of, and by the pain in my jaws, for which I had now no hope of relief, and was in no amiable mood.

As I went back to my escort, the orderly tackled me: "You're a farmer, aren't you? Don't you think your farm is worth fighting for?"

"No, I don't. There's nothing I think worth killing men for."

"No, but other men are fighting for you."

"Are you fighting for me? Am I asking anyone to fight for me?"

"I don't reckon a man like you is worth his salt."

"And I don't reckon you're worth much, attacking a man before you know anything about him. If I were free and we were back in New Zealand, you wouldn't dare to speak to me like this."

I suppose I looked pretty savage. I know I felt it. He paled and retreated before me, his bluff simply fading out. This episode, retailed in the guardroom with much enjoyment by the escort, strengthened the belief generally held in the camp that I was too violent to be allowed out of irons—this belief originating in the fact that I was never seen except in hand-cuffs. The military police enjoyed these stories and I don't believe made any attempt to contradict them.

I had visitors, many of them, and in one respect I gained by it, as the cell was too cold for them and I had to be brought out into the passage to talk to them. On the other hand, I found it very hard always to have to be ready to answer questions, state my case, and stand up against argument, no matter how I felt, no matter how little inclination I had for the task. My opponents were many; they relieved one another and came fresh to the fray. I was only one and often far from fresh. Moreover, they were physically comfortable, while I was the reverse, and often so cold, stiff, and weary that I could hardly drag my tired brain to the encounter.

Several chaplains came. The first was of the confident type. He said he had been asked to come and see me. He thought it a great pity that I should take such a stand and refuse non-combatant service, which, he said, he was sure the authorities would agree to if I offered something of the kind. In that case there would be no need for me to take life, which he understood I objected to doing. "And as for not wanting to do anything in the army, when the State is at war you can't avoid taking part in some way."

"That may be true," I said, "but, at the same time, leading the life one has always led and taking part in the military machine are two very different things. I object to governments forcing the people of a country under conscription to murder the people of another country. I am making my protest against it in the best way I can. War is an evil thing, should be done away with, and I believe *can* be done away with. It seems right to me to stand out against it and I *intend* to stand out against it, no matter what I suffer, even if they kill me."

He said there were plenty of people who did things they didn't like and went through with things when they were doubtful about them.

I replied that I knew there were plenty of people who didn't stand to their convictions, but that was no reason why I shouldn't, and for some people to stand by their convictions might help others to do the same.

"And what influence do you think you are going to have on others, shut up in prison, where no one will ever hear about you?"

I said that I hoped some people would, and that I spread my ideas amongst the people I came in contact with, no matter where.

He concluded by saying that he hoped, for my sake, that I'd see reason.

Most of the chaplains argued on these lines. One man, however, was obviously not easy in his mind, though he had been sent to convince me of the advisability of taking on some form of service. He began by saying he was sorry to see me in this condition. I told him that he did not need to be sorry for me. I was standing to my convictions and trying to practice what he preached from the New Testament.

"Do you, then, base your objection on religious grounds?" he asked.

"I base it on the fact that war is evil. It is murder and I object to murder and to people being forced into doing it. Feeling as I do, it is right for me to fight it as I am doing."

"But," he said, "you have made your protest. Why not cease before anything more is done to you? Some of your companions have done so, and those who have not, who knows what will happen to them?"

I said I was not concerned with consequences, but with making my stand against what I believed to be wrong. What I had suffered and probably would suffer had nothing to do with it.

Was I so certain I was right in the matter? he wanted to know. "The question of war is a very difficult one for many people. It is a matter for very careful consideration. You should go into it and look at it from all sides."

"I went into it very thoroughly years ago, and when war came I had made up my mind very definitely about it. You say that some of my mates have given in? If they have, it was because of the force used against them. Do you justify that? And having heard what I have said, and knowing that I should be acting against my conscience, do you still advise me to cease to stand by my convictions?"

In the end he said he could not advise me to. I think they all felt at a disadvantage in urging me to give up my stand and that hampered them in argument; for they never seemed, for some reason, to put up anything really strong against me.

This was not the case with the non-spiritual officers, who were hampered by no scruples of that kind. They were entirely concerned with trying to force, persuade, or entrap me into offering to undertake some form of service in the army. It was useless for me to say that I had already stated my case, that I was still of the same mind and did not intend to take on any form of service whatever. I had to go into it over and over again, with variations according to the arguments put up.

One day I had a new type of visitor. The guards brought in a man to see me.

"Here's a man just back from France," they said. "He's one of the best men we have. He's been through the whole thing, and can tell you all about it."

He came in, a good type, intelligent and clear-headed. We talked on very friendly terms together. He wanted to hear my point of view, he said. He had been at the Front for three years, mostly in the front lines.

"And all the time I've been passing through stages, 'til now I've come to about the same position as you. I believe war is a bad thing, and if there is any possible way of getting rid of it, we ought to take it. I don't say I've quite the same attitude as you have, but I don't find anything to disagree with in what you say. What surprises me is that it's taken this experience to bring me to this point of view, but you've reached it from the start. I think the stand you're taking is perfectly right."

As he came out they asked him: "How did you get on?"

"All right," he said. "He's a very sensible chap and I'd like to have another talk with him. The only difference between us is that he's known from the start what it's taken me three years to learn."

The guardroom was only a small building and when the door of the partition between the guardroom proper and the passage in front of the cells was open, as it usually was, everything that was said could be heard through the whole place. After my visitor had gone I heard an officer ask the Sergeant in the guardroom: "How did that man get on with Baxter?"

"All right, sir. He came out saying he agreed with every word that Baxter said."

The officer made a sound of annoyance. "That'll never do," he said.

The guardroom listened to the arguments, and as a general rule it was considered, as far as I could gather, that I had the best of it. My official title used at times to cause confusion. I overheard one man in the guardroom say to another: "Did you hear what the C.O. said? 'It would be better if neither side wins the war.'"

"Go on, did he say that?"

And there was much amusement when it was realized that it was I and not the Colonel who had expressed such sentiments.

When I first came into the clink I was told that, since I had left New Zealand, two more of my brothers had been sent over and were now in France. I also heard that all objectors were being sent from New Zealand.* I thought it might quite possibly be true, at least about my brothers, but I couldn't find out that anyone had seen them, though many had heard about it. In the end I found out that it was not true, that no more objectors had been sent out of New Zealand

---

*There were seven Baxter brothers: Archie, Jack, Mark, Hugh, William, Donald, and Sandy. All but Mark, who was married, were arrested. No other objectors were transported from New Zealand.

after us, the experiment having given far too much trouble to be repeated.

I was taken down to the Stores and web gear* was offered to me. An officer, who was present for that express purpose, ordered me to pick it up. I refused. The next day I was brought before the Commanding Officer for summary of evidence preparatory to a court-martial, on the charge of refusing to obey an order. I was asked if I had any comment to make. Yes, I had. Though no communication had been allowed by the authorities between New Zealand objectors and sympathetic organizations in England, Quaker publications had somehow found their way into the camp and had been given to me. These leaflets gave technical points that might be of use to an objector at his court-martial, and they now proved useful to me.

"I want to make it clear that I would not have taken the gear in any case...."

"Yes, yes, that's all right, go on with what you have to say."

"... But the officer, in telling me to pick up the gear, did not say: 'I order you.'"

It worked. The charge was a washout, and for the present at least we were no nearer a court-martial than we had been before. The officer taking the evidence leaned over to Falk, who was in charge of the escort, and asked in a low voice: "Why is this man always in irons?"

"We don't dare to take them off him, sir," he replied.

"Is that so?" said the officer and looked again at me. I dare say I did look rather rough. Hair just beginning to grow after a short crop and a stubble about an inch long—for they didn't give me a shave very often—do produce an uncivilized appearance, enhanced, moreover, by wearing irons. I remonstrated with Falk after we came out. "What made you say that?"

---

*The arrangement of straps and belts that holds a soldier's equipment in place.

He laughed. "It's the truth, isn't it? You heard the Adjutant's orders. We're not allowed to take them off."

"But he took it that I was violent."

"Of course he did, and so does everyone that sees you."

He told the story afterwards in the guardroom amid much laughter.

I was taken to the Stores for the second time and the same procedure was gone through again. This same officer, with furious emphasis, shouted: "I order you to pick up your gear." I refused as before. I was brought before the Commanding Officer and heard the evidence read. Had I any comment to make?

Yes, I had. "I would not have picked it up in any case, but when I was ordered to pick up the web gear I was in irons and therefore unable to pick it up."

This was final. They made no further attempt to proceed with the court-martial. I have never been able to understand the matter. Did they want to court-martial me or did they not? It seems an extraordinary thing that they should have overlooked so obvious a fact as my inability to pick the thing up.

It was a very cold night and I was making my tea last as long as I possibly could, for I dreaded the hours between tea and bed-time. The guard, standing waiting with the handcuffs, grew impatient.

"Come on, hurry up! I can't wait here all night. If you've not finished you'll have to go without."

It was as if he had touched a spring. All the pent-up irritation of those days and weeks of cold and cramp and ceaseless strain, with toothache to add an edge to it, broke over me like a wave, irrepressible, uncontrollable. I turned on him, "You're treating me worse than a dog! Keeping me shut up in this cold without a chance to stretch my limbs! And as for putting those things on, you only do it because I allow you to. You couldn't if I didn't."

"Couldn't I?" he said. "We'll see about that," and made for me.

We scuffled round the cell and he soon found it was not the easy job he had thought it. He shouted for help. Two more guards came in and then a third. The cell was far too small for so many men. They got in one another's way, banged into the walls, and knocked one another down instead of me, and for quite a while had no success. In the end they would inevitably have got the better of me. They got me down on the floor, winded, and sat on me, trying to get a handcuff onto one wrist. At that moment Falk came in. He stood looking at us for a moment.

"A bright lot you are," he said. "Four of you and you can't put one man in handcuffs. Leave the man alone," and to me: "Come out and have a warm at the fire."

"You're not fair to us, Sergeant," the men said, "another minute and we'd have got them on him. You were just a minute too soon."

I came out panting and warm for once. The remains of the guardroom tea still lay on the table. As I had not been able to finish my own I cut myself a slice of bread and took it over to the stove to toast. They all laughed.

"Isn't he a hard case!"

The excitement of the struggle died down. I began to feel rather ashamed of the undignified and inconsistent position my irritation had led me into.

"I'm sorry this happened, Sergeant," I said, "but he caught me on the hop."

"You don't need to be sorry. Anyone can understand a man feeling like that. No one thinks any the worse of you for it."

It was true. Even the guards I had struggled with disclaimed any feeling of resentment against me for it.

I was much in favor that evening. Falk became most friendly. "Don't call me Sergeant, call me George," he said, "and I'll call you Archie. I hope they don't beat you," he went on. "I don't believe they will. I knew from the moment I set eyes on you that the game was no good, and I could have told them that all this business of trying to force you to give in was a waste of time."

He became even more pressing in his offers of friendship. "I hate to see a man shut up like without one bit of pleasure. I'll tell you what I'll do. I'll take you down, one of these nights, to a girl I know."

I did not grasp his meaning at first and thought he was suggesting a social call. He soon enlightened me.

"Mind you," he said, "she's not one of the kind that takes every Tom, Dick, and Harry. She's very particular and only takes officers."

"You're not an officer," I said. He smiled complacently. "I'm specially favored."

"And if she takes only officers and the specially favored, what makes you think she'd take me?"

"I'd fix that up all right."

"You're not really serious?"

"Too right I am. I'm in charge here and can do what I like with you. It'll be quite easy to get you out."

I said: "I'm sorry to have to turn down your kind offer, but, seriously speaking, I don't believe in that sort of thing. I think it's wrong to use women like that."

He was hurt. "I only meant to do you a good turn. I hadn't any idea of trying to work anything."

"I know that. All the same I can't accept it."

Falk did not altogether give up hope.

"He says he won't go," he remarked to the guardroom at large, "but we're going some night all the same, even if I have to take him by force. I'll bet he wouldn't resist once he saw her."

I had uncomfortable visions of the figure I should cut,

being taken by force on this adventure. Whether Falk's well-meant designs would actually have been carried out, it is hard to say, for at that moment the Adjutant walked in. Hitherto, when he had made surprise visits during the preceding three weeks, he had always found me handcuffed in my cell. Here I was, at large, in the guardroom. He was far from pleased.

"What is the meaning of this? Why isn't he in handcuffs?"

Falk, taken unawares, lost his usual readiness.

"The guards don't find it easy to put them on him, sir."

"Don't they! I'll soon put men here who will."

This was putting me in a rather unfair position, but I could say nothing. He turned on me.

"As for you, Baxter, I can see it's the limelight you're after. It's glorification you want."

"Glorification!" I said. "There's not much of it about this."

"You know perfectly well you're being made a lion of here. It's high time you were shifted."

The next day he came in with the Colonel and they told me I was being sent to France that day with a draft. Would I promise to go quietly?

"You'll go anyway, but if you won't give your word to go quietly and not take the uniform off, you'll go in handcuffs."

I had already thought out pretty thoroughly the question of wearing the uniform. For three weeks I had worn it, had never been seen without it. Few—only the guards and the officers who had dealings with me—knew that I wore it only because the handcuffs prevented me from removing it. I had therefore not got very far with it as a protest. If I continued to refuse to wear uniform I should continue to be kept in hand-cuffs. I had only had three weeks of it and had found it inexpressibly trying to both body and mind. My strength had been very much worn down by it. Was I prepared to go on with it indefinitely, wearing myself out on that one point? I should be compelled to wear it, whether I refused or not. I had always admitted the possibility of not being able to hold out on that point, if the authorities chose to use certain means. They had so chosen. Would it not be better to use all my strength in concentrating on the main point, the refusal to perform any military service? They could not compel me to do that without my consent. They could regard it as a victory if they liked. It was not going to prevent me from refusing to take part in the military machine. I do not doubt that there are many who will think I was wrong in not continuing to fight on the matter of the uniform. I am not excusing my action, only trying to give my reasons for it. I said I would go quietly and would not take the uniform off, as I realized I was in their power. As for doing anything, that was a different matter. I would keep my freedom of action and my right to refuse to obey orders. They were sending me to France. Well, my mates were there and I felt I should be with them.

I wanted to see Jack before I left, but this was not allowed. I had never been able to obtain any information about him since I had been separated from him, but I felt sure he had not been sent to France or they would certainly have told me.

The draft was drawn up before the door of the guard-room. The officer in charge called out: "Bring him out."

"Just a minute, sir," said Falk. "The chaps want to say good-bye to him."

All the men in the clink, guards and prisoners alike, came up to shake hands with me and to wish me luck. They asked me if I was going to stand out in France. I said, yes, that I would stand to my convictions, no matter what the consequences, in France or anywhere else. They all crowded round the door to see me go and a great cheer rose as I went out and joined the draft. They stood waving to me from the door until I passed out of sight.

6

WE ARRIVED AT Folkestone late at night and waited hour after hour in the streets, in the cold, drizzling rain. While we waited, the officer in charge of the draft came over to me and said it would relieve his mind very much if I would give my word to do nothing rash on the trip across to France. I assured him I would do nothing violent to myself or anyone else, and that, as far as I was concerned, he had nothing to worry about. He thanked me and seemed greatly relieved.

At last a corporal came along and said: "We've found a place."

We were marched into an old building, foul-smelling and dirty. Each man cleared a space enough for himself and we sat on the floor with our backs against the wall. One man said: "What a rotten show!"

Another said: "It's worse outside."

We had marched away from Sling to a lively tune on the bagpipes, but now everyone seemed depressed and gloomy and hardly a word was spoken. After a while we got a drink of tea, which helped matters considerably by putting warmth into us, and, very soon afterwards, most of us were dozing uncomfortably against the walls.

With the first streak of daylight we went aboard. Surrounded by our convoy, we moved out into the Channel. On our right was a large paddle-steamer crowded with Chinese. Some of our men shouted abuse across to them and the Chinese retaliated with equally lurid language, more than holding their end up, with the result that there was a laugh from our side. We made our way across between the minesweepers: a boatload of silent men, overhung with an atmosphere of gloom and tension.

The coast of France rose before us in the winter sunlight, for the day had become bright and clear. After a very brief stay at Boulogne, which afterwards I was to know better, we proceeded in motor trucks to Etaples, reaching it about mid-day. I wandered about the camp, getting my bearings. Two German airplanes were circling, like silvery fish, high above in the blue sky out of range of the anti-aircraft guns, while puffs of smoke showed where the shells were exploding harmlessly far below them. A little dog had appeared from somewhere and was inviting me to have a game with him, when I heard my name called; looking round, I saw Patton and Harland, two of the *Waitemata* deportees. They took me to a hut where I got some food, and I gave them an outline of my experiences since I had left them at Capetown. They were able to give me information about some of the fourteen. Three, my brother being one of them, had been court-martialed and sent to a military prison in France. Briggs had been separated from the others, and they had heard that, as he continued to refuse orders, he would probably be shot. They themselves had taken on ambulance work. Patton told me he had been sent to a compound and put on No. 1 Field Punishment, and had been struck by a guard.

I was brought before Colonel Simpson. He asked me the usual questions, and I explained my attitude and gave my reasons for refusing to serve. He told me that some of the objectors from New Zealand had been sent to a military prison.

"There's a Baxter among them; your brother, is he?"

"Yes, my brother."

He said he would not like to have me sent to a military prison.

"Those places are run by the lowest type of men in the army, and I know the brutal methods they use. They'd probably kill you."

He showed me a letter which he said he had received from one of the men in prison, offering to come out and do ambulance work.

"Of course, we know what that means," he said. "It's the treatment they've had in prison. I told them to write to me if they had any communication to make. I'm going down there in a week or two, and I expect to find them all of the same mind."

Such bitterness and anger surged up in me that I had difficulty in controlling myself. He would not like to have me sent there! And these others, mere boys, thought likely to be more amenable because of their youth, delivered over to ruthless brutality. Had he no feeling for them? No, only satisfaction when he thought the methods had been successful. I afterwards heard from my brother Sandy just what those methods were. On arrival at the prison, having refused to work, he was sentenced to three days in irons in the punishment cells on bread and water. At the end of the day the irons were removed, but his arms, powerless after twelve hours behind his back in figure-eight handcuffs, were entirely useless. One of the warders came into the cell, and, his jaws slavering and the saliva dribbling over his chin, gave him a frightful grueling—taking care, however, never to give him a blow that would knock him completely out. He was told, and he knew it was the truth and no idle threat, that he would get it again and again, on and on, without end, until he gave in. He told me, too, of an Australian soldier who came into the prison while he was there, a splendid physical specimen, full of pluck and of a manly spirit of independence. He told the other men when he first came in that nothing on earth would make him give in to the bullying and brutality prevalent in the prison. They wondered what would happen. He vanished into the punishment cells. After some time had gone by they used to hear his screams. At the end of a fortnight, he came out, his magnificent physique gone, his nerve gone: a cringing, abject creature, eager to jump at the slightest word from the guards, who used to amuse themselves by demonstrating the lengths to which he would go in the completeness of his subjection.

One of the New Zealand generals is reported to have said that they did not intend to shoot objectors as that would make martyrs of them. When a man is dead he can suffer no more in this life. But when he is delivered into the hands of men who will use any means to break him into subjection, his life, whether he stands out or whether he does not, can be made unendurable. There were many such prisons in France. The men sent to them were not criminals, but the military machine required these places for the maintenance of army discipline.

"It is not our intention to shoot you," Simpson went on, "but of course, if you are sent up to the Front and refuse service there, it's hard to say what will happen to you. Conditions are different up there."

He showed me a long list of New Zealanders who had been sentenced to death, and in quite a number of cases the note was added: "Sentence duly carried out."* He said he was

_____
*This was probably a bluff, however five New Zealand soldiers *were* executed, all volunteers: four for desertion, one for mutiny.

not going to require anything of me at present, but would send me up with a draft to Abeele. He would be following in a few days; I was to explain when I got up there that nothing was to be done with me until he arrived.

We went up to Abeele by train. The soldiers on the way up were friendly to me as always. At Hazebrouck we saw, close to the railway, three enormous shell craters, the first we had seen in France. They were still a novelty, but we were soon to make closer acquaintance with them, where men were glad to crawl into them for shelter, and to see nothing else for miles.

On arrival at Abeele, I was handed over to the military police. The sergeant who took charge of me was a man of Belgian extraction, of gigantic build and most rugged countenance. As soon as I entered the guardroom he seized me in his giant grip and, turning my face to the light, roared: "You refuse to fight? They'll waste no time over you here. If you don't toe the mark, you'll be bloody well shot."

After some consultation he took me over to a hut filled with men. He led me in and, by way of introduction, shouted: "Here's another like these chaps we've been shooting here of late. A bloody C.O.!"

He left me, and as his footsteps died away along the duck-walk,* a hum of curses directed at the military police ran about the hut. In five minutes I had plenty of friends and not a man said a word against me.

Next morning I did not go on parade and was sent back to the guardroom. I told the police what Colonel Simpson had said. They consulted an officer, who said I could go back to the hut and wait until the Colonel arrived.

Headquarters were in an old Belgian farm homestead and part of the building was still being used for the farm operations. I was under no restraint, so I went all round the place,

*A corduroy walkway constructed of wood laid transversely.

taking stock of everything. I went into the sheds where girls were attending to cows, up into the lofts where men were dressing hops, and out into the field where men were turning over the rich brown earth with their one-horse plows. I asked a great many questions, and although most of these people (not having much English) were uncommunicative, I found some who were ready to talk, and even in the space of one day I gained a great deal of information as to their way of living, their outlook on life, and what they thought about the war.

After a few days the Colonel came up and I was brought before him. He asked me again for a statement of my views and I put them as clearly and briefly as I could.

"Do you express these sentiments in the hut?" he asked.

"Yes, when I am asked I give a free account of my experiences and my views."

"And how do the troops take it?"

"The troops show me nothing but friendliness."

"They are only carrying out the order I gave them, but it's not in the interest of discipline to let you remain in the hut."

Turning to the police, he said: "Take him to your quarters and see that he has a chance to shave and blacken his boots and clean himself up, and if he wants to go to church on Sunday, let him go. He can go out for a walk if he likes, but he must not go into the hut."

It was not very long before the police were as friendly as the men in the hut had been, all except Booth, the provost sergeant, who was always cold and aloof. One of the police would say: "Sergeant, can I take Baxter out for a walk?"

"Do what you like with him. It's nothing to do with me," would be the reply.

Some of the police were so friendly that I almost doubted their sincerity it seemed so remarkable, but there was really no question of it. When I met some of them up at the lines afterwards they were as friendly as ever. Of course, I don't say these were the regular military police. They did not like the job.

One day the officer, who walked through at inspection time, looked in my face with such a friendly smile that I couldn't help returning it. Then he became very gay, and holding me by the hand and calling me Mr. Baxter, declared that he was prepared to do anything on earth for me. Was I quite sure I was all right in every way? If there was anything I wanted all I needed to do was to say the word and he would do it for me. When I thanked him, he became more affectionate still and began to try to embrace me. But those who were with him thought it was time to interfere and led him away, still trying to talk to me.

I was provided with a beautiful new web equipment, which I refused to accept. It was left hanging in one of the rooms at the police quarters. The young Belgian giant said to me: "Look, if you don't want that web gear, how about giving it to me? My own is old and shabby and this is a stunning rig-out. What about an exchange?"

I said it was nothing to me if they filled the guardroom with military equipment. He could take the lot as far as I was concerned. He thanked me effusively and seemed to regard it as unheard-of generosity on my part. After that, he, too, was very friendly to me.

I had several interviews with Simpson and various attempts were made to induce me to take on something. I was taken down one day to a parade held for the conferring of decorations. I don't know from whose brain the idea emanated, but it was evidently thought that the sight of all these men receiving honors from the hands of the High Command might stimulate my ambition and cause me to accept service in the army in the hope of like rewards. The military policeman in charge of me asked me what I thought of it all. I said I was not much impressed.

"Would a cup of coffee impress you more?"

"It certainly would."

"Then come along and I'll shout you one."

Another time a sergeant took me along to an enclosed yard where a little scratching of the ground had taken place and suggested that I should plant and cultivate cabbages in it for the troops. I knew that the whole thing was absurd and was only being used as a means of working me into taking service in the army. The place was not suitable for any kind of cultivation. My refusal, however, greatly angered the sergeant. He had had two brothers killed, he said, and here I was, refusing even to assist by growing vegetables.

"You're nothing but a rotter," he said, "and I've no time for you at all."

I said I was sorry, but I hoped he might some day understand what I was fighting for.

At one of our interviews, Simpson asked me if I had religious views. I said I did not belong to any organized Church, but that it seemed to me the teaching of Christ was entirely against war or taking any part in it. But even if that had not been so I would still consider I was right in taking my present attitude. He said he did not suppose that anyone could say what would have been Christ's attitude in war. But anyway this war was a man's war, that was how he looked on it.

Finally he said: "If you won't do anything, my hand will be forced and I shall have to punish you. For your own sake, Baxter, for my sake, for everyone's sake, for Heaven's sake, do something."

I was formally given an order which I refused, and was again brought before him. He sentenced me to twenty-eight days No. 1 Field Punishment, together with the usual stoppage of pay, which did not concern me as I had never had any pay.

"If you take my advice," he said, "you'll obey orders now.

WE SHALL NOT CEASE

The place I am sending you to is hell." He also told me to write to him at once if I had any communication to make.

I was examined by the doctor as to my fitness to undergo the punishment.

"I don't believe you are fit," he said, "but I am going to pass you as fit. You're such a damned fool you deserve all you get."

An escort of military police took me down to the punishment compound at Oudredoum, two or three miles away. The compound was on flat ground, about a quarter of a mile from a railway siding. It consisted of an enclosure about half an acre in extent, surrounded by a barbed-wire fence; it contained a large dug-out used for the quarters of the camp, N.C.O.s, and the cookshop, two tents in which the men slept, and two or three wooden cells against the fence.

I was handed over to the sergeant who was preparing to take the men out on their job of filling in shell holes. He gave me an order which I refused. The sergeant-major in charge, on my refusal being reported to him, said: "Leave him here and I'll see to him later when I have more time."

Afterwards he called me into his dugout and had a long conversation with me. He said he did not like putting men on No. 1 Field and was not doing it at present to the other men, but his orders were that if I refused to obey I was to be tied up. I told him I had never obeyed orders in the army, but had simply gone wherever they chose to take me. I would never take anything on, I said. We talked for hours. He showed interest in, and sympathy with, my views and the account I gave of my experiences, and was ready to argue in a friendly way, without trying to force or entrap me into admissions. He said, finally, that he would think the matter over and see me next day.

The following morning the sergeant asked me if I would go out with the working party. When I replied I would not, he pressed me no further. The sergeant-major in charge had another talk with me. He had thought things over, he said, and was not going to punish me. I could go outside the compound and do what I liked. He would only ask me not to go further than the railway station.

I walked about the place within the prescribed quarter-of-a-mile radius. Sometimes I went to the siding and watched the loading and unloading of trucks. I saw practically nothing of the other men. They were out at work all day, and at night I slept in a hut attached to the cells, the tents being already full. The food was about the same as what the troops got in the lines.

This state of things had lasted a few days when an officer arrived at the compound and interviewed me. Finding that I was not being punished, he was exceedingly angry. I was not justifying my existence, he said, and "should not be permitted to live."

I replied that I understood from a military point of view his saying that I was not justifying my existence, but that it was going rather far to say, on that account, that I should not be permitted to live. This made him still angrier.

"I'll have you shifted at once to a place where you will be adequately punished," he said. "I'll see to it that there will be no more of this sort of thing."

A police escort arrived from Abeele and took me to another compound, not far from Dickebusch, known as "Mud Farm." The sergeant-major from the Oudredoum compound accompanied us, walking with me while the escort walked behind. He was gloomy and abstracted and hardly uttered a word for the greater part of the journey. We came to a little *estaminet* at the roadside, and he shouted me a cup of coffee. At last he burst out as we approached the compound: "This has been a hard business for me, having to bring you to a place like this. I believe it's a damned hard show at any time, and if you refuse orders here, well. . . . You do intend to?"

"Yes, I do intend to fight out to the last."

He took my hand. "Look, Baxter, you are in for something here. I believe what you say. I know you intend to stick it, and I hope you are able to. Nothing would give me greater pleasure than to hear that this crowd had failed to break you. Good-bye and good luck."

He turned back here, as we were close to the compound, and left it to the escort to hand me over.

The officers' quarters stood on one side of the road by which we approached. On the other side of the road was the compound proper, nearly twice the size of the one at Oudredoum. At the left as one entered the gate was a building containing stores, cells, and guards' quarters. In front of the building were the tents where the men slept. To the right, from the gate, was the cook-house, and at the end of it, the latrines. Right at the other end of the compound stood the tents for the German prisoners who were run in in batches to spend one night there on their way to the base. The whole enclosure was about an acre in extent, but enough barbed wire was used in making it secure to fence a fair-sized farm. A double row of barbed-wire entanglements surrounded the whole enclosure. A further row ran round the two tents in front of the guard huts, and, inside that again, each tent had its own encirclement of wire. A lieutenant of the Imperial Army and a New Zealand sergeant were in charge of the compound. Coming along the duckwalk from the gate I observed a long row of stout, high poles to the right. These poles were used for the infliction of No. 1 Field Punishment.

Handed over to the sergeant in charge, I was searched and stripped of everything except the clothes I stood up in and my two blankets. No prisoner was allowed to have a knife or razor or any sharp instrument of any kind.

"The other men are out at work," said the sergeant, "but I

can give you a job helping in the cook-house in the mean-time."

"I don't obey any military orders," I said. "It's for refusing to obey orders that I've been sent here."

"Then you'll have a rough spin. You'll get No. 1 when the other men are at work and on pack drill. Better think it over."

"There's no need for me to think it over. I'm not taking on anything."

"Right-oh," he said. "Come along. I've got my orders." He took me over to the poles, which were willow stumps, six to eight inches in diameter and twice the height of a man, and placed me against one of them. It was inclined forward out of perpendicular. Almost always afterwards he picked the same one for me. I stood with my back to it and he tied me to it by the ankles, knees, and wrists. He was an expert at the job, and he knew how to pull and strain at the ropes until they cut into the flesh and completely stopped the circulation. When I was taken off, my hands were always black with congested blood. My hands were taken round behind the pole, tied together, and pulled well up it, straining and cramping the muscles and forcing them into an unnatural position. Most knots will slacken a little after a time. His never did. The slope of the post brought me into a hanging position, causing a large part of my weight to come on my arms, and I could get no proper grip with my feet on the ground, as it was worn away round the pole and my toes were consequently much lower than my heels. I was strained so tightly up against the post that I was unable to move body or limbs a fraction of an inch. Earlier in the war, men undergoing this form of punishment were tied with their arms outstretched. Hence the name of crucifixion. Later, they were more often tied to a single upright, probably to avoid the likeness to a cross. But the name stuck.

A few minutes after the sergeant had left me, I began to

think of the length of my sentence and it rose up before me like a mountain. The pain grew steadily worse until by the end of half an hour it seemed absolutely unendurable. Between my set teeth I said: "Oh God, this is too much. I can't bear it." But I could not allow myself the relief of groaning as I did not want to give the guards the satisfaction of hearing me. The mental effect was almost as frightful as the physical. I felt I was going mad. That I should be stuck up on a pole suffering this frightful torture, a human scarecrow for men to stare at and wonder at, seemed part of some impossible nightmare that could not continue. But at the very worst, strength came to me and I knew I would not surrender. The battle was won, and though the suffering increased rather than decreased as the days wore on, I never had to fight it again.

The poles were in full view of passers-by in the road. By turning my head a little—the only movement I could make—I could see them as they came from one direction towards the gate. Then they passed out of my line of vision. Peasants came by in carts and on foot, people from the small towns round about—Belgians, I suppose. The civilian population, one and all, went past with averted heads, never looking in my direction, as long, at least, as I could see them. But the men in uniform, whether on foot or not, always looked. Cars went by full of officers staring with all their eyes, often slowing down and almost stopping behind me, to get, I suppose, a better view. It is difficult to know what conclusion to draw from these two contrasting modes of behavior. I hated the staring and much preferred the civilian attitude. But, as it afterwards proved, one at least of those who looked, looked to some purpose.

Towards the end of the afternoon, in the small corner which was visible to me of the enclosure on the other side of the road, heads began to appear and disappear with great rapidity and much blowing of whistles and roars of "Double,

double!" resounded from the same quarter. After some time
the sergeant came over and released me. I set out to walk to
the tent without waiting, as I afterwards learned to, for the
slow and painful return of the circulation to my numbed
limbs, and immediately fell. I struggled on again somehow
and, stumbling and falling, managed to make my way to the
tent. By the time the other men came in, I had pulled myself
together, determined to show no sign, if possible, of what I
was suffering. They were exhausted from pack drill. Doubling
round a yard, with eighty-pound packs on their backs, was
very hard on men after a day's work on starvation rations.
They were in no gentle mood and cursed the N.C.O.s, the
whole military outfit, the war, the world, and its rulers. There
were several Clydeside workers amongst them. One whom
they called Jock was the chief and the lawgiver in the tent.
Next to him came Scotty, also a Clydesider, a much younger
man. The two were devoted to each other, but Jock snubbed
Scotty continually, while Scotty grumbled and criticized him.

Jock looked hard at me and asked: "What's been your
trouble? Overstaying leave, I suppose?"

"I'm here," I said, "for refusing all orders in the army. I have
done so consistently for the last twelve months. I have never
taken on anything and have no intention of doing so."

"On what grounds?" he asked.

"On the grounds that war is a bad thing and will destroy
the human race. I believe that if enough people in each country stood straight out against war, the governments would
pause and be compelled to settle their disputes by other
means. I also believe that the peoples of all nations are naturally peaceful until they are stirred up by the war propaganda
of the governing classes. When the workers of all countries
win their economic freedom, governments won't be able to
set them on to murdering their fellows."

"Are you a Socialist?"

"Too right I am." There was such a rush to shake my hand that we all went down in a heap.

"Well," said Jock. "I'm proud to shake your hand, but I can't say I welcome you to this dog's den of a place."

Soon afterwards tea was brought in by Jock, who was mess orderly for the tent. Tea consisted of a small slice of bread per man, with a scraping of margarine or some kind of fat on it, and a cup of tea. Breakfast was the same. Dinner was a small portion of bully beef and pounded-up biscuit with hot water poured over it, the biscuit still retaining its rock-like consistency. On this diet the men had to do a hard day's work, often with pack drill at the end of it, and every two or three days two hours of No. 1 Field in the afternoon. I got the same food as the other prisoners. It was little enough and did not suffice to keep up one's strength under punishment. The whole time we were, all of us, almost mad with hunger. The German prisoners got porridge. Thin, watery stuff as it was, how thankful we would have been for it! The system at that compound was designed to break the spirit of the strongest: and for anyone refusing orders, as I did, the punishment was intensified in proportion.

Every evening we were searched and the tent was searched for contraband such as food, tobacco, or implements with which we might have cut the wire. In spite of these precautions and the fact that he was always escorted by a guard when bringing meals to the tent, Jock, from his position as mess orderly, did sometimes manage to convey to us prohibited articles of food slipped to him by the cook, who was also a prisoner. On the evening of my second day in the compound, just as I was able to gain my legs and was making my way slowly and painfully to the tent, Jock brushed against me and I felt a slight tug at my tunic. When I got back to the tent I found a pepper tin full of hot tea in my pocket. That tea was worth all the world to me at that moment.

"You shouldn't run risks for me, Jock," I said to him afterwards.

"Never fear that, boy," he replied, "my hands are far quicker than yon loon's een.* Allow me," and he managed it again several times without being detected by the guard.

One night after tea had been brought in, Jock rose and looked out of the tent door to make sure there would be no intrusion by the guards—they could hear what we said if we raised our voices and would shout to us to cut it out if we became too loud—and produced about a quarter of a pound of cheese. With an implement that he had fashioned out of some piece of tin he cut it into cubes about the size of dice and shared them round. We said we didn't want to eat his rations.

"It's all right; it's buckshee,"† he said, and described how the cook had given him the tip and he had managed to slip it off the table when the guard was looking the other way. Scotty, though he swallowed his cube, ridiculed Jock for insisting on sharing so small a quantity. Jock said it was a matter of principle. Scotty said the principle would be all right if there were more cheese. Jock said: "Principle is principle in much or in little, but I'll take no more backchat from you, so shut up."

Scotty obeyed.

The tent accommodated twelve men when it was full. We slept on the floorboards wrapped in our blankets, a hard bed for anyone as stiff and sore as I was.

After breakfast in the morning, the other men went out on their job of filling in shell holes, usually at some distance from the compound, and I was left alone in the tent. The gate in the wire round it was left open and I walked in the enclosure containing the two tents until the sergeant came for me. Usually I did little more than an hour on the post before

---

*That fool's eye.
†Free; an extra ration.

dinner, though sometimes the sergeant chose to come earlier and then I had longer. In the afternoon I never did less than two hours and sometimes as much as three or even four. One day I was put on shortly after dinner. The other men went out to work, accompanied by their escort. The sergeant disappeared, the guards also, and as far as I could see, not a soul remained in the compound, though, as I could not see behind me, there may have been someone there. Hours went by. No one came to release me and I began to wonder if I were to be left on all night. At last I heard voices at the gate, and the sergeant came, hurrying for once. The others told me that he had met them at the gate.

"Surely you must be late," he said to the N.C.O. in charge of the party.

"Yes, we're very late."

"And I've left that man on all this time," exclaimed the sergeant.

Jock said to me one night: "There's something about your philosophy I don't quite understand. We've got to go through hard punishment here and we'd do anything on earth to get out of it. You get it worse than us, and yet you've only got to say the word to escape it all. What enables you to hold out as you do? Is it religion?"

"I'll tell you, Jock," I said, "the answer is quite simple. Religion, as I understand it, and the foundation of my philosophy, is: Do as you would be done by, and war seems to me to deny that and to include everything evil that is in the world. The only lasting victory that we can win over our enemies is to make them our friends. You asked me what enables me to hold out? Chiefly, my belief that my attitude to war is right, and my faith that I am doing more for humanity than I could do in any other way. My fight is not against individuals, but against systems and conventions. I am doing my bit in the war by fighting the war convention."

I had been several days in the compound when one afternoon, just as we were all going to be put on No. 1, the lieutenant in charge came over to have a talk with me. He took me round behind the buildings, out of sight of the poles. He asked me a few questions and, after listening to my views and an account of my experiences, he said: "We all know that war is bad and that it would be a great thing if it could be abolished, but what can a small minority do?"

"What can small minorities do? They can spread their influence, they can grow until they become majorities. You are an Englishman and must know how many times in English history that very thing has happened."

He laughed and admitted that it was so and gave some instances. In the course of the conversation, he asked me what sort of time I was having.

I said: "You are the officer in charge here. You must know what No. 1 Field is like."

"As a matter of fact," he said, "I dislike the whole business so much that I never come near, if I can help it, when I know it's going on."

I said I could understand his not liking it, but what I did not understand was why, in that case, he should take on the job.

He excused himself: "Well, I happened to be offered it. Most jobs in the army are pretty rotten, and one never knows what one is going to drop into."

We had talked so long that I only had about half an hour's punishment after he left me. It was frightful to look at that row of suffering men—men who had committed no crime against society (and if they had, would such treatment have been justified?)—who were social, self-respecting beings, subjected to such a horrible and degrading form of punishment. That in itself, apart from anything else, would have been enough to make me feel I could have nothing to do with the military machine.

We were released and left, as usual, to make our way back to the tents in our own time. We had just started off when the gate swung open, and in poured a stream of German prisoners with sandbags on their heads, looking about as warlike as a pen of hogs. They were only little boys, fair-haired and blue-eyed, without a man among them, and they were in terror of death. They came running up to us, shouting, "Kamerad! Kamerad!" and trying desperately to tear the buttons off their coats to give to us. They only saw the uniform and did not realize that we were prisoners like themselves. I thought of the adjutant at Sling with his lions and tigahs, and I thought, too, of the sergeant-major at Simonstown and what he had told us. The Germans were rounded up and run into their tents and we went into ours.

"You scored this afternoon by your long talk with the officer," said Jock. "If they manage to break you here, it will be a feather in his cap."

"He'll have to wait a long time for his feather, Jock," I said.

"What do you think of him?" he asked.

"He seems a queer, easygoing devil. I can't quite make him out."

"I'll tell you what I think of him," roared Scotty. "He's a bastard. He may be easygoing in a way, but he knows how to keep a soft job, and he's responsible for all the muck that lousy sergeant rubs into us here."

"Shut that gab, or I'll shut it for you," hissed Jock. "We'll have the guard in here and you don't want that."

Jock asked me one evening: "If they send you up to the front line, what will you do?"

"I'll continue to fight as I am doing here."

"It must be hard to fight without support. I don't know what will happen to you in the end."

"It doesn't matter what happens to me, and, as far as support goes, whenever I have a chance of making myself understood, I get it every time. You men have already been at the Front. Tell me, would those armies which are fighting and slaughtering one another, take long to fraternize if their respective governments called a halt and came to terms?"

And the whole tent answered as one man: "If the war were called off, they'd become friendly in no time."

"You are certainly doing something," said Jock. "You've made a difference to this place. What I'd like to know is, what are all the preachers and parsons doing? In peacetime they preach: 'Thou shalt not kill,' and 'Love your enemies,' and all that, but when the nation goes to war, what happens to them?"

"Aye," said Scotty, butting in. "I know that crowd. It's bread and butter they're after. Preach love and goodwill in peacetime and in wartime mount a recruiting platform and preach hate and bloody murder. They're the same in all countries, supporters of the capitalist system, hounding the workers on to kill one another. Tell me if they're not on the side of the wealthy and the powerful every time?"

"I'll tell you what I think about that," I said. "I've no time for recruiting parsons myself, but I know there are good men, in the churches and out of them, who have courage and sincerity, and my hope is that in the future they will get together and inspire more and more people to see the futility of war and to bring pressures on governments in the interests of world peace."

"Hope!" said the only other New Zealander in the tent, who always looked on the dark side of everything. "There is no hope of altering things for the better. It doesn't matter what people try to do. We're like rats in a trap, and no matter what you try, there's no way of getting out. What good do you think you're doing by your fight? Nothing, only making things worse for yourself."

"It may look hopeless," said Jock, "but I'm convinced that

it's not. I've not lost my faith in the common people and I believe that, when they come to understand better, things will change."

He began to talk about his life in Glasgow and what a wonderful woman his wife was. He had the greatest admiration for her even when, as sometimes happened, she criticized him pretty freely. Jock never believed in despondency. Newcomers, sunk in the depths of despair at finding themselves in such a dreadful place, would be greeted with: "Well, mate, what's your trouble? Overstaying leave? Ever been in an outfit like this before?"

And when they had indignantly denied this: "Well, you'll find the best brains in the army here."

Even if, at first, they looked on him with scornful wonder, as if cheerfulness in such a place were blasphemy, it was not long before they fell in with his ways and found things the better for it.

I had been in the compound some little time when Kirwan, one of the fourteen deported men, was brought in under escort. I hardly knew him, for he had been separated from us on the *Waitemata* after the first few days. As he was not in the same tent with me we did not get much opportunity for conversation, for when we were on the poles we seldom exchanged a word. He did tell me, however, that this was not his first experience of Mud Farm. He had served a previous sentence there and had spent part of the time in the punishment cells on biscuits and water.

Soon after his arrival the weather became very cold and rough. With the change in the weather the other prisoners were no longer put on No. 1, but Kirwan and I were, morning and afternoon, as usual. I thought nothing could make the punishment worse than it was, but I soon found that cold, stormy weather greatly increased the suffering. I began to find it almost impossible to sleep at nights from restlessness and pain. I was alternately burning hot and shivering with cold, and the constant pain in my joints woke me whenever I did doze off from exhaustion. The kindness of the other men in the tent I can never forget. They insisted on making my bed, and often, I know, would put their own blankets and over-coats under me to make it a little easier for me. One man, a Canadian, was particularly friendly, and ever since, because of him, my heart has warmed to Canadians.

It is hard to say if I would have lasted out the whole of my sentence—I was going down physically every day—if some-thing had not occurred a few days before it was up. A day came, one of those days in early March that outdo the middle of winter in cold and storm. There was a blizzard blowing, with the temperature below zero and the snowflakes freezing as they fell. I was not expecting to go out, for I did not imag-ine that they would tie us up in such weather. I was mistaken. The sergeant called me out. As we had never been allowed to wear our overcoats when on punishment, I did not suppose I should be allowed to take mine now, and I left it in the tent. Outside, I found that Kirwan had risked it and worn his. I thought of asking to go back for mine, but on second thought decided not to, as the result would probably have been that Kirwan would have been told to take his off.

We were tied to the poles as usual. The sergeant and the guards retreated to the guard hut, where we could see them through the open door—which faced away from the wind—sitting over a red-hot stove. Soon a smell of coffee came to our nostrils and we knew they were enjoying their morning cup. The storm blew in our faces and in a very short time we were white with snow from head to foot, the flakes freezing so rapidly that they clung in spite of the gale. The cold was intense. A deadly numbness crept up until it reached my heart and I felt that every breath I drew would be my last. Everything grew black around me, although I was still quite conscious. Suddenly, loud voices sounded behind us and an angry, red-faced New Zealand sergeant appeared beside the poles.

"What's all this bloody business?" he shouted. "At first I thought they were posts, but when I went closer to look I saw the hats. I never saw such a damned thing done in all my life."

Here the compound sergeant, who had come hurriedly out to meet him, made some remark that I could not hear.

"I don't care who they are or what they've done," the stranger shouted. "It's what you're doing to them I'm concerned about. I didn't think men would do such a thing. I'll make it known everywhere. Take them off at once."

The sergeant drew him aside for a moment and I heard no more. Then they came back and the visitor stood by in silence while we were released. Afterwards, the two sergeants walked away across the road in the direction of the officers' quarters. That ended it for us. We were not put on again.

Two days later a police escort arrived to take us back to Abeele. I would have liked to have said good-bye to the other men, but they were at work when the escort arrived. As we made our way towards Abeele, one of the military police remarked: "There's been a great go about you two men at camp. Everyone's talking about it."

One of the first men I met on arrival at Abeele was the sergeant who had cursed me when I had refused to plant cabbages. He came up to me and asked me to forgive him for what he had said. "I didn't understand then. I do now. I've changed my mind."

"There's nothing to forgive," I said. "I never had any feelings against you. I knew you didn't understand. I'm glad you've changed your mind, but do tell me what has made you change it?"

"It's Mud Farm! Mud Farm!" he said. "I know—we all know—what you suffered down there."

I held out my hand and he took it. We stood silent for a moment. His face showed his feelings. I said: "We won't talk about it just now."

We took leave of each other and I did not see him again. He, and others like him, made me feel my fight was not in vain.

The next morning Kirwan and I were taken before Colonel Simpson. He glanced at me and said: "Well?" I looked straight at him and answered: "Well?"

"They tell me," said he, "that they can do nothing with you down there."

"You sent me there to try to compel me by force to submit to army discipline."

"I have tried hard to consider you, but my hand has been forced. I once had hopes of you. It is most regrettable that you should take up such an attitude. What do you think will happen to you up at the lines if you won't submit?"

I told him I had no intention of submitting and was not concerned about consequences.

He said: "Well, I hope it is so."

This remark puzzled me at the time and still does.

He turned roughly on Kirwan and ended by saying: "I have no time for you at all. When you get up there and are ordered to dig, take my advice and dig. If you don't, you'll be hammered black and blue from head to foot."

"That's the way he always goes for me," said Kirwan, when we were outside again. "He seems to have a set on me."

"It's meant for me just as much as for you," I said.

As I knew we were to be sent up the lines the next day, I thought I should try and give my people some idea of what had happened to me so far and what my attitude still was. This might be the last chance I should have of writing,* I said:

_____
*March 5, 1918

I have just time to send you this brief note. I am being sent up the lines tomorrow. I have not heard where Jack and Sandy are. As far as military service goes, I am of the same mind as ever. It is impossible for me to serve in the army. I would a thousand times rather be put to death and I am sure you all believe that the stand I take is right. I have never told you since I left New Zealand of the things I have passed through, for I knew how it would hurt you. I only tell you now, so that, if anything happens to me, you will know. I have suffered to the limit of my endurance, but I will never in my sane senses surrender to the evil power that has fixed its roots like a cancer on the world. I have been treated like a soldier who disobeys (No. 1 Field Punishment). That is hard enough at this time of the year, but what made it worse for me was that I was bound to refuse military work, even as a prisoner. It is not possible for me to tell you in words what I have suffered. But you will be glad to know that I have met with a great many men who have shown me the greatest kindness. If you ever hear that I have served in the army or that I have taken my own life, do not believe that I did it in my sound mind. I never will. . . .

I cannot think how I could possibly have imagined that such a letter would pass the censor. The strange thing was that it did, and reached my people in New Zealand unaltered. I wrote the letter in the police quarters, and took it down to the censor's hut. I was wearing neither hat nor coat. I laid it on the table in front of him. A sergeant who was present roared at me: "Salute the officer!"

I refused: "I have never saluted anyone in the army and I don't intend to."

"If you never saluted before you'll do it now," shouted the sergeant. "Salute the officer."

I turned to the censor who was sitting behind the table: "I refuse to salute you, not because I have anything against you personally, but because I object to military service. I have no doubt I would respect you if I knew you as a civilian, but I have no respect for your rank as officer. I consider myself a civilian, and do not salute officers. Besides," I added, "I am in undress."

The officer had a kindly smile and most intelligent face and it now lit up with a smile. But he said not a word.

"Shall I crime him, sir? Shall I make out a crime sheet,* sir?" asked the sergeant eagerly, disregarding my remarks about being in undress.

"Not as far as I am concerned," the officer replied.

The sergeant nearly choked. "He's refused an order, sir. Shall I take him to the guardroom, sir?"

The officer, still smiling, answered: "I think he'll find his way there without you," and I left, without an escort.

On my return to the guardroom, the military police dressed me fully, put a box respirator† on me and took me along with Kirwan to a small structure like a telephone booth, in which we went, one after the other, through a gas test. Back again in the guardroom, they tried to force a rifle with bayonet fixed on to me. I refused, and when it was forced into my hands I stuck the bayonet into the floor and told them to go and ask the Colonel if I was to be given a rifle. They came back with the information that the Colonel had said I was on no account to be given a rifle.

---

*A list of misdemeanors and crimes that were attached to a soldier's record.
†Gas Mask.

7

THE NEXT MORNING Kirwan and I were handed over into the charge of Booth, the provost-sergeant. He took us by lorry* to several places behind the lines. At one of these he stopped and, telling us that we were to have no food, he made us stand behind him while he ate his dinner. When we arrived at the hut where we were to spend the night, we found Mark Briggs. I had always hoped to strike him somewhere, but had ceased to expect it. We exchanged experiences. In Sling, his had been much the same as mine. Kept in irons for the whole of his four weeks there, for the last five days he gone on a hunger strike. He had then been sent to France. At Etaples, refusing to parade, he had been left unmolested—first in the guardroom, then in the mess orderlies' tent—for seven weeks. Sent up to Poperinghe and refusing orders there, he had been sentenced to twenty-eight days No. 1 Field Punishment. He had served six days in the Oudredoum compound, three of them in punishment cells, when one of the New Zealand generals had arrived at the compound and interviewed him. The general told him, after

*Truck.

he had talked with him for some time, that nothing would be expected of him for a time at least. For more than two months he had remained at the Stores, doing nothing and going about as he pleased. Two or three days before, this policy had been changed, and he had been told he was to be sent up the lines. This sudden tightening of the tension came hard upon him after two months respite.

Early the following morning Booth came into the hut and gave me an order, which I refused. He was standing in front of me with a disagreeable smile on his face, giving no hint of what he was about to do. Suddenly, he struck me a blow on the jaw; I was not expecting it and fell heavily. Before I could get back on my feet he struck me again, and then again and again, every time I tried to rise. When I at last managed to gain my feet, he had left the hut. After a few minutes I went out and met him just outside.

"Have you got anything against me that you did that just now?" I asked him. He was plainly taken aback at my speaking to him in an ordinary way. "No, I've nothing against you personally," he said. "I've got my orders and I'm carrying them out."

"That's all I wanted to know."

One of the camp cooks was standing at the cook-house door. He came out and cursed me soundly. He had probably seen and certainly heard what had gone on in the hut. The thuds, bangs, and crashes as I came in contact with the walls and the floor must have been audible for some distance. At first I could not distinguish what he was saying, but the last of it I made out. He roared at me: "You'd let the sergeant hit you! You won't obey orders! You're worse than a bloody Hun!"

He was too far away and I did not feel up to explaining things then, so I let it go.

Soon after this, Kirwan, Briggs, and I were taken before the Colonel in command at that place. He told us we were being sent up the lines and, if we did not obey orders there, we would have to take the consequences.

On our arrival at Belgian Chateau, a short distance from the shell-ruined town of Ypres, we were brought before an officer whose name I never heard. After asking us a few questions, he told us in a half-facetious manner what he thought of us.

"Up 'til now you've been having a pretty easy time, and I expect you know all the *estaminets* about. But things are not going to be so rosy for you in the future. As for you," he said turning to me, "you should be more modest in expressing your views. Instead of saying 'No' and 'I won't,' you should say: 'I can't.'"

My stiff and swollen jaws made speech so difficult and this irritated me so much that I have no doubt that I was abrupt and defiant.

We were all three left together in a hut and then taken, separately, before Captain Phillips. He argued with me at great length. I felt utterly disinclined for argument. It was one of the penalties to the fight, and a hard one, that I had to stand up to argument at times when I had no inclination for it and when I knew I should only make a poor showing. Phillips told me he knew all about us and that we were not regarded as sincere objectors by the New Zealand government. As not one of us belonged to a sect according to whose tenets war is forbidden, we had no standing. I pointed out that the New Zealand government knew long before they deported us that we were determined to stand out against all military service. It was useless for anyone to say that we were not regarded as objectors. After some discussion Phillips complained of my lack of cheerfulness. Why did I need to be so short and disagreeable in my replies? I said: "This morning, before I was brought here, I was knocked down several times by blows in the face from the provost-sergeant in charge of me. My jaws are so stiff that I had hardly use them to speak; and you expect me to be cheerful! Under such circumstances would anyone be?"

He said I had brought it on myself. He went on to say that as I refused to do work under military control he would give me a chance to do something not under military control. He then gave me a document which stated that I was not under military control but under his direct control.

The following morning I was taken over to the Otago camp, a short distance away on the other side of Ypres, and presented at headquarters as soon as I arrived. I showed Phillips' document. They took a copy of it and said they would wait until he arrived. I knew perfectly well the whole thing was farcical, but I wanted to see what they would do. Phillips arrived later in the day. He told me I could do just as I pleased, that I would not be given any orders and was to be addressed not as "Private" but as "Mr." He took me over to where some men were filling in shell holes with a plow. He asked me if I would direct them in preparing the land for potatoes. I would not need to do anything myself, only direct them. As I was a farmer I would know how to do this. I knew how absolutely absurd it was to think of growing potatoes there. When I passed by some days later the whole place was plowed up again into holes by shellfire. I asked Phillips whose control I should be under. His own private control, he said. I asked him if he really expected me to take this thing seriously. I had presented his document as soon as I arrived, I said, and had immediately been attached to a battalion, which showed that the thing was worthless and would be ignored by the military authorities. As for saying I would be doing this job under his control and not under that of the army, he must know himself that it was nonsense. He was angry and showed it, but he continued to argue. To hold such views, he said, I must have lived in a very small and isolated community, completely out of touch with the views and outlook of the rest of the world. I was, in fact, mentally abnormal.

"You admitted it yourself yesterday," he said. "You told me you were not normal." I felt this lawyer-type attempt to twist what I had said to be most unfair. He went on to say that I had become so used to standing out that I went on with it automatically without thinking the matter out or realizing that I was doing no good by it now. And because I had held out so long I found it very difficult to give in now. But that was just what he wanted me to do.

"Do this difficult thing and you will have won a greater victory than you think. It is only your pride that is holding you back. You have made your protest. You are getting nowhere with it now."

They were taking into consideration the fact that I had refused orders so far and were not asking me to fight. But I was in the army and whatever I did or said did not alter that fact. In the army, men often had to do what they very much disliked doing.

"For example, if I were called upon to make one of a firing party to shoot my own brother I should have to do it."

"And would you do it?" I asked.

"Most certainly I should."

"You yourself have supplied me with an argument," I said, "and I am very much surprised that you should say it. That is the very thing that makes it impossible for me to become part of a machine which demands of men that they should do such things with unquestioning obedience. In civil life you would look upon such a thing with horror, but as part of the machine you would do it. That shows how evil the whole thing is." I had several interviews with him. On one occasion he asked me: "You want your nation to win the war?"

"I don't want any nation to win. A decisive victory on either side will mean sowing the seeds of future wars."

"Is that the way you look at it?" he said. "You are an obstructionist and I'd rather see you with your skull knocked in against the parapet than let you get back to New Zealand."

I was surprised at the effect of my words. Would he have been satisfied if I had said I wanted the Allies to win? Then, of course, he would have had an argument to his hand.

"I'm sorry you have such feelings about me," I said. "I don't feel that way about you."

He said he would now let me know that they had had instructions from New Zealand about me.

"These instructions are very harsh. I would not like to tell you how harsh. One thing I can tell you is that violence will be used against you if you continue to refuse orders."

"It has already been used against me and I am prepared for it."

He said I must know myself that I would be beaten eventually; I must know that I would be broken.

"And if I *am* broken, what good should I be to the authorities or anyone else?"

"That doesn't concern us. It's your submission we want, Baxter, not your services."

This cut me more than anything else he said. He wanted, he continued, to warn me of the position I was in. If I did manage to hold out, I would never leave the Front alive.

"I know there are people who support you in New Zealand. Don't imagine that your story will ever reach them. Whatever happens to you, you will be reported as having died or been killed on active service and these people in New Zealand will never know that you had not taken it on."

I believed him as far as the intentions of the authorities went, but I thought all the same that there was some chance of news getting out. Even if I had been convinced that there was no chance at all of anything being known, I would still have gone on. But I held to that hope in spite of Phillips.

At the close of our second interview, he had me sent back to Belgian Chateau. Here Booth took charge of me again and informed me immediately that I was to have no food until I obeyed orders. A day or two previous to this, I had met a cousin of mine. He did not understand my attitude, but, moved by the clannishness which remains with Highlanders, even in the Colonies, he gave me ten francs. I went over to the Y.M.C.A. hut and purchased a cup of cocoa and some biscuits at the canteen. Booth had seen me coming away. He now searched me and, finding the change from the ten francs, removed it and everything else he found in my pockets. I protested. "It's my own private property. You've no right to it."

But he was not bothering about rights in his pursuit of his objective, my submission, and I got no redress. He watched me carefully and prevented me from getting anything. On the evening of the third day without food, desperate with hunger, I went across to the sergeants' mess which was close to my hut, when I knew they had just finished tea, and asked the mess orderly if he had any tea left over. He said he had had orders not to give me anything, but, all the same, he would put a can outside the door and I could help myself. I had just dipped up a little tea in a tin from the bucket when Booth came up, snatched the tin from my hand, and threw the contents on the ground.

The cook's dugout was in the bank of a ditch near the hut I occupied. The next day the cook called me and asked if it was true that I was getting no food. I told him how long I had been without anything.

"I can't see a man starve," he said. He showed me a sort of ledge in the wall of the cook-house, and told me to watch when he gave me the tip and he would try to slip something through an opening in the wall onto the ledge. I did as directed, and in a very short time he slipped out a large, newly cooked rissole. I have never seen a rissole since without thinking of that one and the man who made it for me. It warmed me and appeased my hunger, so that I felt I could go another three or four days without food. I don't know which pleased me most, the rissole or the manly spirit of the cook. He gave me something again the following day.

Afterwards, when I saw him lifting heavy buckets of water up a slippery bank, I helped him. An officer saw this and remarked to me that he had seen me helping the cook. I explained that any such action on my part was voluntary, that I would do as I thought fit in any emergency, but would not be a cog in the military machine.

It was at this camp that I was under shellfire for the first time. Ypres was being shelled continually and the places round about got their share of it. It had happened that all the shells I had seen up to that time had exploded at some distance from me. One night I was alone in the old tin shed I inhabited when there came a terrific roar overhead, followed by a crash and the sound of splinters falling on the iron roof. I sat on the floor of the hut and counted the explosions. There were intervals of a few minutes between them and they all seemed exactly alike, except one which made a dull, heavy thud. This one, I afterwards heard, had struck the mule stables. There were nine shells in all.

At the first crash, when the splinters began to come through the roof, I had a sensation as though all my flesh were hardening, a sensation that never came again at any subsequent experience, and a tense feeling of the need of some kind of action and of suspense between shells, owing to the fact that several minutes elapsed between each explosion.

Next morning I had the luck to find an iron ration* in an old disused hut. This was indeed a win. I had lit a small fire to boil some water for tea. As usual, a dog had made my

*K rations.

acquaintance, a little fox-terrier. He was waiting for his breakfast, knowing that if I had food he would have his share. I heard a voice I knew and, turning round, saw Kirwan approaching.

I called out to him: "We are just about to sit down to breakfast. You are welcome to join us if your teeth are good."

I noticed his hands were shaking.

"Are you cold?" I asked. "Come along, a drink of hot tea will warm you."

"No," he answered, "I'm not cold, but I'm fairly knocked out, that's all."

I realized how far out one can be in judging by appearances. I had been inclined to think that Kirwan felt hardships and ill treatment less than others because he expressed himself so little about it. I made jokes about the picnic party, wishing to cheer him. But he was not in the mood for jokes.

"You're a queer chap," he said, "laughing and joking like that. I don't know how you can. I can think of nothing but standing out and what I've got to go through."

"That's what's the matter with you," I said. "Try to keep it off your mind. I'd go mad if I thought about it all the time."

In the afternoon we were sent back to the Otago camp, but not together. The hut I was in was close to the one used by the sergeants—so close that I could hear them talking. I could pick out Booth's voice, loud and excited. "He was dragged up the duckwalk and thrown into shell holes 'til he was mud from hell to breakfast time and still the bastard wouldn't give in. I never thought he'd hold out."

Another voice said: "A pity to see such courage wasted."

"Courage!" said Booth. "Only a madman would stand what that man stood."

"Will he live, do you think?" someone asked.

"That's for the quack to say. We're waiting for his report now."

I left the hut and asked one of the men: "Has anything happened to Briggs?"

"Yes," he said, "he was dragged along the duckwalk and was badly injured. He's lying in the medical hut now."

On my way over to the hut I met Booth, who told me that Briggs was in a very serious condition and was not expected to live. If he did, he was to be shot. I entered the hut. My old comrade was lying on a bunk. One glance at his face was enough to tell me the seriousness of his condition. It was the face of an old man, pale and sunken. He looked up at me and smiled, and the smile had something almost of triumph in it.

"You've had a rough time?" I said.

"Look," he said, "I made up my mind at the start that I'd go through with this if it cost me my life and I'm going through with it. They can't do anything more to me now, unless they kill me."

Bit by bit, at different times, I got from him what had happened. He had refused to walk up to the front trenches when ordered to do so that morning by Captain Stevenson. Booth, who was present, had dragged him outside by the wrists, tied a long piece of cable wire round his body under the arms, and with the aid of three other men, dragged him at the end of the wire for about a mile along the duckwalk. Battens were nailed across the boards of the duckwalk at short intervals and, to make walking easier, netting wire was nailed over them in parts. Any clothing that protected his back was soon torn off, leaving it exposed naked to the battens and the wire. They dragged him like this for about a mile until they came to a large shell hole, full of water. Here they stopped and Booth asked Briggs if he would walk now. If not, he'd go into the shell hole. On his saying that wherever he was going he was not going to walk up, he was thrown into the shell hole, pulled through it by the wire, dragged over the ground until they came to the next shell hole, and pulled through it in the same way.

When they got him out on the bank at the other side, they took him by the shoulders and tipped him head over heels back into the water. Just as he had managed to get his head above water and was trying to get his breath, Booth fired a handful of muck into his mouth.

"Drown yourself, you bastard," he said. "You've not got your Paddy Webbs and your Bob Semples* to look after you now." They dragged him out, along the ground to another shell hole, through that in the same way, and a short distance further along the ground. Then Booth asked him if he would walk up if they took him back to camp and gave him a change over a fire. Briggs said: "Never, as long as I draw breath."

He agreed to walk back to camp. When he came to try, he found he was unable to and he was half carried, half dragged back by two of the men, suffering greatly in the process. Back in the hut they took his clothes away, dressed him in a fresh shirt and trousers, and left him lying on the floor of the hut under a pile of blankets. After several hours the doctor had come in and exclaimed: "What a damned shame!" when he saw the state of Briggs' back.

Then the orderlies had been told to get him to the medical hut and try to get some of the dirt out of the wound.

While I was in the hut, the doctor came in again. I prepared to leave, but he stopped me.

"Don't go. You can watch me dress his back."

I don't know why he wanted me to stay. I concluded that he hoped to frighten me into submission by the sight of Briggs' condition. I may have been wrong. If it was so, he was sadly mistaken. My feelings were very far from submission

---

*Patrick Charles Webb (1884-1950) and Robert Semple (1873-1955). Both men were major players in early N.Z. trade union/Labour Party politics. Both were imprisoned for opposing conscription.

and fear as I looked at the huge flesh wound in Briggs' back and hip, about a foot long and nearly as wide. In spite of the attempts of the orderlies there was still a great deal of dirt in the wound. It was ground too far in to be easily taken out. That a man with such injuries should not be sent to hospital was an unheard-of thing. For reasons which, after what Phillips had told me, were fairly obvious, Briggs was never sent to hospital. That he pulled round and recovered up to a point was certainly not due to the necessarily very scanty and inadequate attention he received, but to his own good health and excellent constitution. From the very first day he had to drag himself outside to the latrines, though utterly unfit to do so.

When the doctor had finished I left, for Briggs was too exhausted by the dressing for further speech. Booth met me outside and asked me: "Well, have you seen your friend?"

"I've seen some of your dirty work."

"That's the way you'll be tomorrow."

I went back to my hut and was standing in the doorway when I saw two men limping across the parade ground to where some limbers* stood. They began to push one of them, but appeared unable to move it.

"We're stuck! Give us a push, digger," they called out to me.

"Wait a minute," I said, and walked round the building, where I came suddenly on a sergeant-major, peeping round the corner to see how things were going. He saw the game was up and called out: "Come along," to the two men. They went off without a sign of a limp and the limbers remained there until we left.

Next morning Booth came into the hut, accompanied by several men. "Now, Baxter," he said, "we are going to give you the father of all hidings before you leave this hut."

"All right," I said, "if those are your orders, I'm ready. But

---

*A two-wheeled vehicle, originally pulled by horses, behind which was towed a field gun.

hold on a minute! What are you giving it to me for? What am I doing?"

Surprisingly enough, he fell flat. Up until then he had been all excitement and eagerness, his mouth open, and his lips showing moist and red against his olive skin. He rushed outside calling to the other men to bring me along. Shortly afterwards I saw him again, this time stalking Kirwan, his face lit again with the same sinister eagerness. He struck Kirwan a blow on the jaw, sending him into a clay bank near which they were standing. Kirwan picked himself up and joined me and we were taken together for some distance to where the Entrenching Battalion was working near the front lines above Ypres. Here we were separated and Booth took me before Captain Stevenson. He told me that my position was serious and the sooner I realized it the better. There was no more room for argument. Nothing I had to say mattered as I was not now in New Zealand, but in France, under shellfire. Booth now took a hand. They were not going to "philander about" with me any more. I was to be given one more chance to obey and if I didn't take it I was to be shot. The shooting would be done on the spot, by him. He had his revolver ready. He gave me an order. I refused. I don't know why he didn't shoot. I think it was not only bluff, and that at one time he meant to, if I refused.

He struck me on the mouth and ordered me again. I refused, and he struck me under the jaw, making my mouth bleed. He kept on saying: "Do it! Do it!" and I kept on saying "No!" Each time I said it he struck me again in the face or body.

"You only need to work for half an hour," he said, "and we'll guarantee to send you sixty miles behind the lines and give you some job at the Base."

"Yes, I suppose they would," I said. Some shells fell a short distance away.

He paused to remark: "Those are the damned things you're frightened of. You don't like them, do you?"

"Who does like them?" I asked. "Do you?"

He made no answer. Angry shouts began to come from the men—there were hundreds of them—working round about. Booth stopped to see whether the anger was directed against himself or me. Not being sure, he started again. This time they made their meaning clear by shouting: "Stop it! Do it yourself, you lazy big bastard!"

He stopped at once.

"I suppose that encourages you," he said, angrily. "I'll take you where you won't have any sympathizers," and he took me at a rapid pace some distance away to a pillbox.

Standing behind this, we were out of sight of the men and he began again, this time punching me in the ribs—hard punches delivered in rapid succession, very many in the same place. The effect of this, besides being exceedingly painful, was irritating to the last degree. The desire to strike back was difficult to withstand. But I had made up my mind to stand it without retaliation and stand it I did. I regarded it as part of the violence which the New Zealand government, according to Captain Phillips, had issued instructions to use against me.

At last Booth desisted, tired out. He took me up to Captain Stevenson and they discussed me for some time. Finally, they decided to send me into the front trenches. A message was sent to the officer in charge there. The messenger returned with the reply that the officer refused to take the responsibility. On this, Booth asked Stevenson if there were any place, near at hand, that was being heavily shelled. He pointed out an ammunition dump at some distance. The Germans had got the range of it and it was being heavily shelled at intervals of about twenty minutes. He told Booth to take me across to it and leave me there. Booth told me to stay there and not to move from where he had placed me. As he hurried away, leaving me standing by the dump, he called back: "I hope a shell gets you and blows you to your Maker."

I stood waiting. I could see him and he, of course, could see me, though he was well out of range. Suddenly, firing began again and the shells came thick and fast. I was in the midst of a storm of spouting, belching, mud and fire and flying fragments. The shells seemed to strike everywhere except where I was. I believe that if I had moved at all from where I stood, I should inevitably have been killed. If the dump had gone up, I should have gone with it. I stood and waited for what seemed inevitable death. I remember that I had very strange sensations, probably due to my overwrought condition. The normal instinct of self-preservation seemed for the time being to leave me entirely. I felt quite calm and peaceful and saw everything round about bathed in a bright white radiance. The whole thing felt strange and unusual, but not unpleasant. I never felt the same again when I was, at subsequent times, under heavy shellfire.

The shelling went on for some time, then ceased. Booth came hurrying back. It needed no white light to make him appear unusually pale. His lips were trembling as he tried to speak.

"Why did you stay there? Did you want to commit suicide?"

"You told me to stay there."

"You're not usually so ready to do what I tell you," he remarked with something like his customary sneer. "Anyway, I believe you're mad, and I'm not going to have anything more to do with the job. Believe it or not, it's not been a job I've liked."

I don't know that I believed him. If he had succeeded in his object, he would have liked the job well enough. As it was, failure made him believe he had not liked it.

I remained with the Otagos and had nothing more to do with him. From that time I received the same food as the other men. A day or two later I saw him departing, no doubt to make his report to Simpson. He had done his best and the unpopularity he had gained in the doing of it—the camp cooks collected and counted him out the night after he had dragged Briggs—probably seemed to him most unjust. After all, he was only carrying out his orders.

Next morning I was standing in the hut alone, the others having gone out, when two men came to me and said they had orders to take me up the lines.

"Very well," I said, "you can take me up, but I'm not taking on anything when I get there."

All the way up they discussed my position and attitude in a very friendly manner. When we got up there the men in charge of me were told by a sergeant that he intended to give me no orders, and, on their asking what they were to do with me, he laughed and said they could show me round. Accordingly, they took me about and told me the names of the different positions, pointed out the crooked German lines and many gun positions. We spent the whole day in this way. They showed me how to duck from shell explosions and how to take cover when it seemed that none existed.

At night I went back to the camp. At this time I always slept and got my food with a hutful of men—seventeen of us there were. I found them perfectly friendly. The position of the objectors was the talk of the camp and the anger of the men was aroused against the provost-sergeant.

For a day or two Kirwan and I had been separated and I did not know what was happening to him. An officer came to me and told me Kirwan wanted to speak to me privately. He asked me to promise not to influence him in any way that would thwart their purpose. I gave no promise, but shortly afterwards Kirwan appeared. He told me he was being sent to a Base hospital. Before he went he wanted to know from me whether his action would make things worse for me. What could I say? I knew what he had suffered at Mud Farm and at the hands of the military police. I knew the condition he was in. What could I tell him but that he was not to worry, that his going would make no difference to my position? I would get on all right, I told him, and he should do whatever seemed best to him. Things looked pretty dark. Briggs disabled. Kirwan sent away. I would be left alone to be slowly ground down by the military machine. But I could not tell him this. I put a cheerful face on it and I think he went away less troubled than when he came.

A little later, Captain Phillips spoke to me, asked me how I was getting on, and offered to get me a hut to myself. I would be much more comfortable, he said, instead of being crowded in with other men. This seemed true. I thought that at least for sleeping I would be better by myself, so I thanked him and accepted his offer. I was surprised at such consideration for me on his part, as he could not have been at all satisfied with the way things were going. I was still holding out. However, perhaps his feelings towards me had undergone a change. I moved into the other hut. I was not alone for most of that night, for two men came over and talked into the small hours. The next morning one of the men from the hut I had left came over to me.

"You come back to us," he said. "Don't stay in a hut by yourself."

"Why not?"

"Who ever heard of a man being offered a hut to himself? It's all a scheme to get you killed. Never you mind how I know, I do know. Most of us are with you, as you know, but there are some chaps who'd kill you if they thought nothing would be done to them." So I moved back.

The following day Phillips spoke to me again. Why had I

moved? Had I been disturbed? He'd get me a dugout where I'd be certain to be undisturbed. I laughed.

"It's very good of you to take so much trouble about me, but I prefer to be with the crowd, anyhow."

He didn't try any more. I supposed that he wanted to prevent me from spreading my ideas among the troops.

Every day I was taken up the lines by a man told off for the purpose. Up there one day a corporal said to me, handing me a shovel: "Here, get onto this."

Before I had time to refuse, a sergeant said to him: "Here, you get onto it yourself, right now."

The corporal obeyed at once. The sergeant went on: "You've had no orders to deal with him. Time enough when you have."

An officer came up, gave my guard an order, and sent him off. Then he turned to me: "What about you?"

I told him who and what I was and that the man he had just sent away had charge of me for the day. He called him back and asked him if this were correct.

"Yes, sir."

"Why didn't you tell me before?"

"You didn't ask me, sir."

"Of course not. I knew nothing about it. Well, I don't want to have anything to do with the matter. You'd better look after your charge."

One morning I was in the hut alone. The men were all out on the parade ground. I heard a very youthful corporal ask why I was not on parade.

"He ought to be out."

"He's in that hut," said an officer. "You can order him out if you like."

He came in and, with a terrific show of military bluff, asked why I was not on parade. I told him I had never gone on parade and did not intend to.

"If you've never been on parade you're going now," he said, and ordered me out. I refused, and looking at him quietly, said: "Well, I suppose it's your move now."

His fresh fair face turned red. Without a word he walked out of the hut and was greeted with a loud laugh.

A captain—I did not know him—asked me if I had a wife. When I answered in the negative, he said: "Well, suppose you had and you found a German assaulting her?"

"Why a German, particularly?"

"Well, any man, for that matter?"

"I suppose I would act in that case like any ordinary man, but I don't see any parallel between such a case and war."

I was prepared to show him that atrocities are perpetuated as a rule by any armies in occupation of enemy territory during wartime, but he did not want to go on with the argument. If I afterwards had a son, he wanted to know, how would I reply to his question: "What did you do in the war?" This ridiculous stock question always amused me.

"My answer would be," I said, "I did my best to stop it."

He said I was costing the New Zealand government money. I said I had never taken a farthing from them and never intended to. It was not my fault if the nation were wasting money on the war. I was, indeed, very little worried over the question. They were destroying men, body and soul, and that was something that could not be replaced by all the money in the world.

I lived a strange life at that time. I would not serve in the army and yet I was at the Front. In one way I was isolated and alone and yet I lived the life the soldiers did. I lay in holes and trenches with them round by Hellfire Corner, hour after hour, until the shelling slackened or drove us out. I was only seeing a glimpse of the war, but it was enough to bring home to me its terrible reality. I remember before I reached the Front meeting men who had been there and thinking they looked hard and strange. Their faces had a drawn look and they seemed to have eyes like eagles. Now that I was amongst them I did not notice this. They seemed ordinary, but new arrivals looked as gentle as sheep.

I will not attempt to describe the battle front above Ypres, but will try to convey the impression it made upon me. It looked as though a herd of prehistoric monsters had chewed and rooted up the earth for miles around. Not a sign of anything green and not a chance for anything to grow. It was part of the Front that had been taken and retaken so often that it presented an appearance of indescribable chaos. Everywhere there was mud and slush and men always floundering through it by tracks and duckwalks that were always being blown up. I was told that a million men had fallen there. The cemetery of a million men! It was still being shelled and the yawning mouths of the countless shell holes were ready to suck in the living men who moved day and night among them like maggots in the slime.

I would often stand alone at night gazing at the red glare along the Front while everything vibrated to the ceaseless roar of the guns. Thoughts came to me as I stood. Every day the war lasted only made things worse for the world. Victory in the field seemed to me the worst that could happen, no matter which side won—not for lack of patriotism, but because I honestly believed it would be the greatest bar to enduring world peace. At times everything was blackest gloom without one ray of hope. The war might go on for years. I believed it could be stopped any day and that the feelings of all the peoples would be joy and relief. Why should it go on?

I discussed the war frequently with the men I happened to be with. They were not war-minded. I remember one day a padre addressing the troops. As we listened to him, I heard the men around me sigh and murmur beneath their breath.

The padre seemed to be out of touch with his audience and not very sure of himself. He told us that wonderful things would come out of the war, that when it was over we would be free to build a new and better world. Great spiritual blessings would spring from these times of trouble and sacrifice. Rulers were to gain great wisdom and to lead us to a condition of well-being and security that we had never dreamed of in pre-war days. I wondered as he went on word-spinning how much of it he believed himself. It was impossible to tell, for the poor man had not the freedom that I had to express himself. Was there a parson at the Front who dared to preach "Thou shalt not kill," that all men are brothers and God the father of all, irrespective of race, creed, or color, and that things being so, the combatants on both sides should fraternize with the enemy? Or a parson with socialist views who dared to say to the troops that the fact that the imperialists and financiers had fallen out was no reason why the workers should be led into war to blow the souls out of one another? And what would happen to such a man? He would be brought up with a round turn, adjudged a nerve case or a mental case and so rendered harmless. To run the military machine efficiently everyone must be regimented. Beliefs on war or religion matter little, but the expression of them must not be suffered to do harm.

This was the only religious address I remember hearing in France. No padre ever spoke to me personally all the time I was there. My life dragged on from day to day, each day much the same. Rations were often short up there. The other men supplemented them from the canteen, but I was unable to as I had no money, what I had having been taken from me by the police.

Every day I went up the lines with a man in charge of me. One morning we started off, following the duckwalk in a zigzag course among the shell holes. As usual there was a certain amount of shelling going on. At a corner we came to some bodies lying side by side, wrapped up ready for burial. We walked on, glancing at them as we passed. I thought of them as individuals, of what their lives had been before, of the friends and relatives who would, in time, get this news. Not sentimentality, as much as the fact of these corpses lying beside the track. I had felt the same about a dead German we had seen in a shell hole further back, lying with his arms spread wide and the rifle still beside him. Just after we passed the corner, a shell passed close to us and struck a bank a few yards to our left. We were knocked down by something, we did not know what. When the earth heaved up by the explosion had fallen again we pressed on and found that the duckwalk had been blown up in places. Arrived at the brow of a little hill, we—the man who was detailed for my escort and I—found we had lost sight of those in front. We were walking in twos with about ten yards between each pair. Presently we saw some of them in the distance. We left the duckwalk and took a short cut over some low-lying ground to catch up with them. Halfway across my companion shouted "Gas!," adjusted his box respirator, and helped me with mine. I do not know whether it was defective, but I found I couldn't breathe in it, at any rate while I was moving. At the last gasp, my laboring lungs unable to draw another breath, I pulled it off, thinking I might as well take my chance with the gas as die by suffocation then and there. I could smell nothing but there was a dark blue haze floating among the shell holes. The other man persuaded me to put it on again. It was just as bad as ever, but by the time I was forced to pull it off again, we were pretty well out of the area affected by the gas shells. It must, however, have had some effect on me. For weeks afterwards I coughed up black stuff.

We could see the other men going up a hill a little ahead of us. I afterwards heard that that hill was in direct view from the German lines. Shells were bursting between us and the men ahead. We paused for a moment, doubtful what to do, then went on. Shells began to fall behind us. As we hurried up the hill they came thick and fast and gained on us. When we got to the top of the hill, we met the other men coming back. The shelling was closing in on us from both sides. We were surrounded by a perfect storm of shells. We all stood for a moment huddled together, the last thing we should have done. The officer in charge of the party was standing close to me as the storm closed over us and I heard him call out: "Every man for himself!" as he jumped over a bank. I had a quickened sense that something frightful was happening. The earth seemed to be like the waves of the sea, and struck me again and again. I felt a strange swaying motion, another bump and then utter darkness and suffocation. There was a violent tugging at my legs and before I could realize what had happened I had landed head-first in the mud at the bottom of a shell hole. I came out choking and spluttering but able to breathe.

One of the two men with me in the hole—they had tugged me out—plunged his arms nearly to the shoulders into the mud, retrieved my helmet and slapped it onto my head. The shelling was still going on. One of the men said: "Come on, it's no good here," and we scrambled out. I gave one glance up, saw dark fragments falling through the air, and looked down again. We were knocked down several times, but not one of the three of us was directly hit. We came right on a little door that seemed to lead into the earth. It was a small dugout over the top of a shaft. One man was there at the windlass.

"It's no good here," he said. "It won't stand a shell and I am expecting it to go any minute."

He directed us to a place about a hundred yards further on. At that moment a shell almost blocked the entrance. We scrambled out and found the other shelter, a wooden drive with steps leading deep underground. For the present we were safe. The others took out their cigarettes and pushed handfuls into my pockets. I did not know them and I thought it probable that they did not know who I was. I did not feel I could take their help and comradeship on false pretenses, so I told them I was refusing service.

"Don't you worry," they said. "We all know about you," and they offered me more cigarettes.

We stayed there for about half an hour. Then, finding things outside were comparatively quiet, we came out. Stretcher-bearers were working on the ground where we had been. We made for a point where we expected to meet the others, if there were any. We found a few men collected together and shortly afterwards the officer came up at a quick pace. We had been twenty-eight. We were now eleven. He was annoyed. Where were the others? Why hadn't they turned up? They had had plenty of time. Hadn't he given orders to meet at a certain point? They were all silent.

"Didn't you hear my orders?" he asked, addressing me.

"I heard you say: 'Every man for himself.'"

He turned abruptly from me to another man. "Well, where are the others?"

The man hesitated. "The stretcher-bearers would get some, perhaps, I don't know, and as for the others—well. . . ."

The officer's face underwent a rapid change.

"You mean they're. . . . ?"

"Yes, sir."

There was silence for a minute. Then the officer in a subdued voice told them to carry on.

I never saw again the man who had been with me before the shelling. As I now seemed to be in nobody's charge, I went about among the men until four of them told me to come with them. We talked and they gave me more cigarettes. It was the only way they could show their friendliness. It was useless to protest. When they left to go back to camp, I went with them to where a light railway ran down the side of a valley. Shells were falling all around. The men climbed on to the trucks like a swarm of bees. I sat with some others on the engine. Shells were bursting on the line ahead. I was watching the track in front and all at once I saw that it was torn up. There was no time to do anything. The train left the rails and rolled over the bank. The engine came to a halt lying on its side, stuck in the mud. It was a scene of great confusion. A mass of struggling men were trying to extricate one another, and all around the crash of shells. Anything I did at that time was done instinctively as a man, not as a soldier, and was not what the authorities wanted.

At night I would go to the medical hut and talk with Briggs. He was recovering. Before we left, a fortnight after he had received his injuries, he was able to walk up and down a little in front of the hut. Most of the time he lay on his bunk. I brought him all the outside news, wishing to entertain him. But he found it hard to take his mind off his position. In fact, he told me, he had to concentrate all the time; it was the only way he could carry on. On the other hand, I had to think of other things and found it a great relief to do so.

As I talked, a shell screamed overhead. Instinctively, I ducked.

"What makes you do that?" Briggs asked, annoyed.

"It's all very well for you," I said, "you can't get any lower. But I've got accustomed to doing it every day, and I do it automatically."

"You shouldn't go up," said Briggs.

On that matter we never agreed. He thought I shouldn't allow myself to be taken up the lines. It seemed to me that as long as I refused all orders when I got there, it didn't matter. After all, it is only a matter of where one draws the line, and that each individual must decide for himself.

Colonel Simpson came up to the camp and spoke with me. He wanted to know if he could do anything for me. Had I no communication to make to him? No complaints? He said he was tired of this punishment, punishment, and he must see the General about me.

I told him I had no communication to make to him. This was understood between us as being the polite formula for giving in. I was still of the same mind, I said.

"You've got a mental kink," he said.

I told him he could think so if he liked, but that I had no kink. He departed, still talking about "seeing the General."

8

THE YPRES CAMP was broken up and we all moved back to Abeele. A man was sent into the hut to bring me out to join the others. We walked two miles to the railway. I saw Briggs at the station looking completely done. How he had managed to walk those two miles I can't imagine. As we moved away from the Ypres sector going, as I knew, to the Somme, I was only conscious of an intense weariness, an unspeakable longing to rest and be done with it all in this never-ending struggle.

We reached Abeele and I spent the night in a hut with Briggs and some other men. It was a cold night and Briggs' blankets had failed to arrive. I tried to persuade him to take mine but he would not.

The following morning Captain Stevenson came into the hut, followed by four men, and ordered me out on parade. I said: "I never go out on parade."

He ordered me again and I refused.

"You ——," he shouted and struck me in the face, knocking me down. I got up and he ordered me again. I refused. He kicked me and struck me another blow, knocking me down. This time I did not rise quickly, and shouting: "Come on, none of that!" he dragged me to my feet, knocked me down again, and kicked me several times about the body. His anger increased by the murmurs of the men with him, he gave me a final kick, the effects of which I felt for a long time after, and ordered the men to bring me out.

"I'll kill the bastard yet!" he shouted.

They carried me out and laid me down gently on the duckwalk.

"Lift him up as high as you can," he ordered, "and drop him on his back on the boards."

They lifted me high on their arms and lowered me to the ground ever so gently, keeping hold of me all the time. Three times, cursing, he ordered them, and three times they lowered me in the same way to the ground.

It was a brave act on their part, for though technically they had obeyed the order, they were incurring the wrath of the Captain—and there were many ways in which he could make it unpleasant for them afterwards.

Then, at his orders, they carried me out into the parade ground and set me on my feet. But my legs wouldn't support me. I fell and lay against my pack. I felt completely dazed and had little idea of what was happening until Simpson passed along the ranks and came to where I lay.

"What's the matter with you?" he asked.

I answered: "I'm all right."

"Why don't you get up?"

I only wanted to be left in peace. I was silent.

"Hm, mentally deficient," he said, then, shouting, so that the troops could hear: "He wouldn't even cook for his mates; I've no time for him at all."

He passed on.

I do not know how long I lay there. When I looked about me again, the troops had gone and I was alone.

Four men appeared beside me. They had been sent, they

said, to bring me to the camp to which the men had shifted, about half a mile away. If I wouldn't walk they would carry me. I said I would try to walk, and we started off, with a man supporting me on each side and the other two men carrying my kit. They gave me frequent spells on the way and it took us a long while to do that half mile. They took me into a hut, put blankets over me, and brought me a drink of tea. I lay there until some time in the afternoon, when Stevenson came in and ordered me out.

"Are you going?" he asked.

I said "No."

I had no fear of what he might do. Brute force had expended itself, had defeated its own object, and put me beyond its reach. I believe that it always does, but unfortunately those who are subjected to brute force don't know that that point will be reached. One reaches this point; if one went forward to death it would mean going easily out. But coming back from it into ordinary life is another thing. Then one has to pay the price for that immunity.

Stevenson apparently realized that I was beyond his reach, for instead of attacking me, he ordered the men with him to bring me out. They carried me out and laid me down. After a time they took me before an M.O.* in the medical hut. He sat at a table nervously moving things about on it. He gave one quick glance up at me, then down again.

"What's the matter with you?"

"I have not paraded sick of my own accord," I told him. "I have been brought here. I'm bruised from head to foot."

"Have you any complaint to make against anyone?" he asked.

"No."

He pushed a couple of No. 9's† across the table to me in

* Medical Officer.
† A complaint form.

silence. That was all. I never made complaints, for I would have been making them to the men who were responsible for what I had to complain of, and they were looking for me to make them. As far as an objector's position in the army was concerned, he had no rights. He had the rights neither of a soldier nor of a civilian. If I had given in, as was frequently explained to me by officers, I would then have the rights and the protection of a soldier.

I was told that the men who had brought me over to the camp that morning were brought up on the mat for having taken so long to bring me over. They had boldly and openly given their reasons. They described my condition and the treatment that had caused it. Some notice had to be taken of what had been openly stated and a doctor's report had to be obtained. Hence my interview with the M.O.

The next day a man came up to me in a state of excitement.

"You're no good!" he said. "You wouldn't fight! You'd let the officer hit you."

In his excitement, he imagined I was going to strike him. He jumped back.

"No! No! Don't fight me! I'll bring someone to fight you. I'll bring three men if you like." He turned to the assembled men and shouted: "What are we to do with a man that won't fight? In my opinion he's nothing but a bastard!"

Another man came up to stand beside me, and loudly and clearly, in a voice that carried to the outskirts of the crowd, said: "Listen to me. At the time when the National Register was taken in New Zealand, 33,000 men said they would not serve in the army, either in New Zealand or out of it. Where are those men? I was one of them. There are many here. A few have stood to what they said and here is one of them. What has made him stand to it?"

There was a shout of "Guts!" and the men laughed. The

originator of the argument had disappeared. I certainly did not feel overburdened with guts at the time.

The man who had shouted abuse at me the morning Booth first struck me, now came and apologized to me. I had not seen him since that day.

"I didn't know a thing about you that time I cursed you," he said.

I had forgotten all about it. It seemed very remote.

The same day I was taken down to the railway, where we were all crammed into trucks on the first stage of the journey to the Somme. We were packed in, forty men to a truck, sitting so closely together on the floor that it was almost impossible to change one's position. Stiff, sore, and weary as I was, I felt I would have done anything for a place to rest in. The men were strangers to me, but some, at least, must have known who I was.

"About these conscientious objectors," someone began.

"Sh! there's one here," said someone else, and not another word was spoken on the subject.

On the evening of the second day we stopped at a station, but we were not allowed to leave the trucks. All night long we sat in them beside the station. Not until the early morning did we detrain in heavy rain. Water was boiled for tea beside a hedge which bordered a field near the station. Only a cup of tea and a snack. At that point we left the railway and marched through the country by winding roads. As we passed through a village, I noticed the men ahead of me buying food at a doorway. I had discovered twopence in my pocket. Where it came from I had no idea. "This will buy me some food," I thought. But by the time I reached the door, everything was sold out and the French girls had closed it. Seeing a girl standing in the yard of the house, I went over to her and offered the money, asking for something to eat. She said they had nothing left, nothing at all. But I was desperate.

"Give me something to eat: I'm starving," and pressed the twopence into her hand. She went away then and, returning with a biscuit tin, tipped a few biscuit crumbs into my outstretched hands.

I went on with the others. It did not strike me to do anything else. I just went on. We halted for the night. Tents went up and they got busy in the cook shop. I came up with the others and held out my tin. I had received my food with them ever since Booth had left.

"What's your platoon number?"

I knew I was done then.

"I can't give a platoon number."

"Then I can't give you anything," and he turned away.

I should have had to go to an officer and asked to be attached to a platoon, and that would be, of course, the submission the authorities were looking for. I realized that it was now a fight to a finish, and there could be only one end to it, but I made my decision, to fight it out to the end. It was now a very bitter fight. I find it hard to write of it even now. Sometimes—quite often—I was sunk in despair, seeing nothing but utter hopelessness in my fight, in any effort to overcome the forces of destruction. The world would just go on for a thousand years and the effort of man to progress beyond mutual destruction was futile. At times I didn't bother to think about it at all, but just kept on. At first hunger drove me to hunt in tins for odd scraps and the dregs of tea, but after a while I ceased to be hungry and did not do so any more. As my bodily weakness increased I remembered the dead men lying in the mud and thought: "It won't be long now before I'll be with them." I wondered if any of the truth would reach New Zealand. I was not with men I had known before and I was no longer able to explain my attitude and views to them. The authorities, I knew, would put me down as killed in action or as having died of sickness and that would be all anyone would know. But I did not trouble about it as I once had. The men were friendly and filled my pockets with cigarettes. It was a token of kindly feeling, as I knew, but I could not smoke. They did not know I was getting no food and I did not wish to tell them, as their rations were little enough and they hadn't much opportunity of supplementing them.

I have no clear and consecutive memory of that time. It may have lasted a week. It may have lasted longer. I only have a general recollection of growing weaker and of being less and less able to drag myself along. Certain pictures stand out clearly from the mistiness. I was toiling along a road up a rise, having fallen behind the main body of men. A doctor—I think the doctor who had attended to Briggs at the Ypres sector—was standing at a corner, urging on the stragglers pretty sharply. As I came past him he said to me:

"I know how hard it is for you, but try to keep up a little longer and you'll get a spell, up there at the top of the hill," and he pointed to where a windmill stood outlined against the sky.

I struggled on and found a farmhouse up there, and got a drink of water at a pump. Then on again, wearily and hopelessly. As night came on, I found myself with a group of men who had fallen so far behind the main body that they had lost touch with it. When we came to three crossroads they had no idea which way to take. An English officer, passing by on horseback, directed us down a little valley to the left, where, he said, we would find some of our men encamped. We went on to a wood, and there we found that tents had been erected and there were some of our men about.

The others lined up for food. I had not tried again since the first refusal, long before, how long I do not know. But now I thought I should make one last effort to keep life in me. I held out my tin for the last time and met the same answer. I turned away and lay down exhausted on the sodden earth. My head and limbs were burning and I could neither rest nor sleep. My brain was working at lightning speed but the thoughts were confused and incoherent. I can remember in the dim light of early dawn seeing Chinamen lying on the ground like caterpillars wrapped in their cocoons. Then everything was a blank until a time, later in the morning, when I looked round me and could not see a human soul. The place was absolutely deserted and looked to me like a place of the dead. I was clad only in my underclothes and socks. I had no recollection of taking off my uniform and boots or any idea why I had taken them off. I did not at the time, feel much surprised or puzzled over this. Only one thing was clear in my mind: I must catch up with the others. Shells were bursting near at hand and I reasoned that if I went in the direction from which they were coming I would find the other men.

I set out. There did not seem to be any roads. At any rate I found none. I floundered along, falling into ditches full of water and struggling out again until I found my legs would carry me no further. Then I tried to get along on my hands and knees. I came to a large shell hole full of water. To go on I should have to crawl round it. I hadn't the strength to, so I lay down on the edge of the crater and realized that I could go no further. I lay half conscious, without thought. An airplane came down quite close to me, then mounted again and disappeared.

Suddenly a voice beside me said: "You don't want to fall into that," and I saw two Tommies standing near.

I said something to them, but I don't think I made myself intelligible. One of them remained with me; the other went away. After a time he returned with a horse. They put me on its back and set off, one leading the horse, the other holding me on. After some time, I have no idea how long, we came to what must have been an English dressing station. The

Tommies handed me over and I was put on a stretcher out-side. An unknown face appeared above me within a short dis-tance of my own. Startled, I exclaimed: "Who are you?"

"I am Colonel—(some name I didn't catch). Now tell us who you are."

They poured something down my throat and questions were shouted into my ear. I could hear them quite plainly, but it was difficult to answer. They had nothing at all to go on as I had no identity disc. After a time I managed to answer some questions and then they left me in peace to drowsiness and unconsciousness.

Some time in that day the face appeared again and the voice said: "You don't need to worry any more. We have found out all about you."

I had not been worrying and the information did not interest me. Afterwards, I would have given a good deal to know just what they were told about me when they made inquiries of the New Zealanders.

I was given something more to drink and, after what seemed a long time, I was carried out and slid into a sort of shelf. After that there was a continuous rumbling and sway-ing and bumping. It was night when I was taken out and laid on the floor of a large tent. I was given something to drink and began to revive a little and take notice of my surround-ings. I was carried across the road and put into a bunk in a small room. There was one other bunk in it, occupied by an Australian. The orderly in charge of us made a few remarks and then went out, closing the door. I was sufficiently roused to notice that he locked it. At that time I thought nothing of it or of the fact that I should have been kept apart like this with one other man. Later, of course, looking back, I was able to realize the significance of it.

The Australian sat up, groaned, and rose off the bunk. He was a tall man, young and strong.

"Why have you been put in with me?" he asked. "What's the matter with you?"

I told him I had been standing out against serving in the army and had been knocked out.

He stared. Then his face changed and, showing his bandaged hand and arm, he said: "Look here: I don't mind telling you, I did this with my own rifle."

I felt very embarrassed at his confession and did not know what to say. At last I murmured awkwardly: "That's a pity. Do they know?"

"Yes, they know."

It seemed to relieve him to be able to talk about it. He was on the verge of breaking down, wondering what would happen to him, what they would do to him. I let him talk. I felt for him very much. There would be no sympathy for him, no understanding, and his fate would inevitably be hard. Unless people can clear their minds of the war convention they can never have any real understanding of such cases, but will simply dismiss them as cases of cowardice.

At last he said, pulling himself together: "Well, I suppose there's nothing for it but to make the best of it."

My momentary flare-up of clear consciousness was passing: I was slipping back into dreamy semi-consciousness, and I remember nothing more of that night.

I was on a hospital train on the way to Boulogne. Only a very confused memory of the journey remains. I thought I was on a ship. I could feel the motion of the waves. Sometimes I knew where I was. In the early dawn I can remember being carried up a sloping platform and laid down on a floor. Then I can remember no more.

9

I CAME TO CONSCIOUSNESS to find myself lying in bed in what was evidently a hospital ward.* When I had last been conscious of my condition, I had been stiff with mud and dirt under the enwrapping blankets, and very lousy. Now the bed was clean, and, what was more surprising still, I was completely deloused. I had not the faintest recollection of the process by which this state had been brought about, or, indeed, of anything at all since the train. I asked how long I had been there and was told two days. I felt weak indeed, but my head was now perfectly clear and I had no more lapses into unconsciousness. Only too clear; for it was not long before I realized what sort of place I had come to. It was a ward for mental and nerve cases. I never found out whether it was a separate hospital or a special section of a general hospital. In the ward in which I found myself there was a terrific din going on. Men without a vestige of control were wailing and crying over their wounds, in many cases self-inflicted. Others, suffering from delusions, were holding forth on imaginary grievances. One voice rose above all the rest. It

*April 1, 1918.

belonged to a man who had been badly shell-shocked and who was quite oblivious of his surroundings. He would lie for hours at a stretch on the broad of his back, singing until he frothed at the mouth and grew purple in the face. Then the orderlies would seize him and shake him. He would give one blood-curdling yell and stop, to begin again the next morning. It was apparently useless to try to stop him until he had reached a certain stage, and it took him the same time to reach that stage every day. He seemed to compose his song as he went along. Dozens of verses, all variations on the same theme, something like the following:

> *They tried him in the trenches*
> *And they tried him in the air*
> *They tried him in the Navy*
> *And they tried him everywhere*
> *But he didn't like the show*
> *And he said he'd have to go,*
> *And it's ho, your navy,*
> *Your silent navy, Oh!*

He always ended each verse with the "silent navy."

I was greatly distressed at finding myself in such a place. Why should I have been sent there? The doctor in charge came on his rounds and I spoke to him: "Do I have to stay here?"

"Why, does it trouble you?"

"Yes, the noise does."

"I'll have you shifted," he said, and I was taken through a door into what was really only another part of the same ward. I could still hear the singing and the shouting, but the sound was now distant and my immediate surroundings were quieter. The men here were, most of them, able to talk rationally.

The orderlies carried me along to the bathroom. The

sight of my body—emaciated, fleshless, with the skin drawn over the bones—gave me a shock and I turned my eyes away from it in disgust. I was always very cold. I could get no warmth between the sheets, so I slipped in between the blankets, though I knew I was not supposed to, and after one or two attempts to induce me to return between the sheets, they let me alone.

Every day, as he passed my bed, the doctor asked me how I was. "When you are better," he said, "I want to have a talk with you."

The time came. He questioned me. How had I got into such a condition? How had I come by the marks on my body? Had I been blown up by a shell? I hesitated. He was so pleasant and so friendly and I appreciated it so much. Now I would see that friendliness and sympathy give place to cold hostility, judging by my past experience of prison and army doctors.

"Come," he said. "You must try to tell me." I said I had been knocked down by shells but that I had not been hurt. Then I told him what had happened to me. I watched his face. It altered, but not quite in the way I expected. Several times he attempted to head me off, and suggested that I had been in some building that had been wrecked by shellfire. I stuck to my story.

"Do you disapprove of what I did?" I asked.

"I don't blame you at all," he said, "but don't worry over these things. You've been sent in here a sick man, and it's my business to put you on the road to recovery as soon as possible."

I was puzzled. He had not reacted as I had expected and yet there was something about it I didn't understand. The next day he came back.

"Do you know," he said with a friendly smile, "I didn't believe a word of what you told me yesterday. We get so many wild tales in here, all imaginary, the result of delusions. But your papers have just come down and from them I can see quite plainly that you have told me the truth. I am glad to find that you are not suffering from delusions."

It seemed hard to understand, he said, that the New Zealand authorities should have gone to such lengths with me. He hardly thought the British government would have acted in that way.

"It is difficult to see what they expected to gain by it. If they had got you to give in, you would have been of no use to them."

The next day he had a further talk with me. "You are against this war?"

"I'm against this war. I am against all wars."

"I can understand that," he said. "Some people only object to particular wars."

The hospital was a one-storied temporary structure, built round the three sides of a courtyard. There were beds running down the parallel sides. At the end was a wide corridor in which we exercised when we were able to get up, with bathrooms at each end and a passage leading out of it. There may have been wards beyond this. I don't know. The hospital—under the control of the doctor in charge, a mental specialist—was staffed by a surgeon, a matron, a sister, two nurses, and a number of orderlies. The nurses attended principally to the men who were severely wounded, but they also came round and talked to all the patients with whom it was possible to talk, making a considerable difference to the atmosphere of the place. The doctor spent hours every day with the patients, talking at length to some, saying only a few words to others.

One day, when I thought I had sufficient control over my weakness to enter on the subject—the effort of speaking caused the perspiration to run down the backs of my hands, and, try as I would, I could only speak in a hollow whisper—I asked him: "Why have I been sent to a mental hospital?"

"We take all sorts of cases here," he said, "nerve cases, shellshock cases."

"But why should I be considered that sort of case at all?"

"Surely you must know, Baxter, that your nerves were in pieces when you came in here?"

"Yes, I know I was ill, but I'm all right now."

He laughed.

"You're all right here. Don't worry about it. When you come in, we have to go by what those who send you in say, but when we send you out, we don't need to go by it, we can say what we like."

As I grew better I talked with some of the other patients and heard their stories. One of the first men I came to know was a Jamaican Negro named Peter. When he came to my bedside to talk to me, I gave him some of my views on the brotherhood of all men and the wrongness of war and violence. His eyes grew very large and he said with great earnestness: "Yes, shure." He left me and I heard him telling some of his countrymen—there were several Negroes there—something of what I had said. "Now," he said, "I cannot let this good man die," and he went off to the stove and toasted a bit of his bread ration. I told him, when he pressed it on me, that he needed it more himself. He replied that he would willingly go without food for a long time if by that means he could put me on my legs again. Rather than hurt his feelings, I took a little of the toast, and his face lit up with pleasure. He watched over me with great care all the time I was in bed, and when I was able to get up, his joy knew no bounds.

The Negroes there—with the exception of one man who had threatened to shoot his Colonel and one man who was badly wounded and whose story I did not know—seemed to be suffering from an acute form of home-sickness.

They were desperately anxious to get back to Jamaica and their families.

There was a German prisoner in the ward who had been in a starving condition when he came in. The orderlies used to pile up his plate with food the other men had left, with the result that he was improving every day. One of the Negroes, called Henry, used to watch this going on. One day, after he had watched the German for some minutes in silence, he rolled his eyes and shouted: "It's nothing but the height of damnfoolishness! If that man fills out, he'll kill everyone in the place."

One man I talked with seemed to be perfectly normal and well. He told me he had gone to the Colonel and asked for leave to go over to England to place certain verses of Scripture before Lloyd George. He was convinced that if he could only point these verses out to Lloyd George, he, L.G., would then know how to stop the war, and would, of course, immediately bring it to an end. He had been put under observation and had still clung to his idea, with the result that a label had been tied round his neck with "mental" on it and he had been dumped here. He was simple-minded, and earnestly religious, no more mental than he had ever been. Thousands of people have thoughts like his, but unlike him they don't think them strongly enough to put them into action, especially not in the army, so they don't land in mental hospitals.

There were a number of men there with self-inflicted wounds. Some of them were quite uncontrolled and cried continually over their wounds and their future fate. The man in the bed next to me had a very bad hand. It was being drained with tubes and the dressing was a painful process. His nerve was completely gone and he would cry and call out the whole time it was being dressed. One day the surgeon, while he was dressing the hand, said to him: "You wouldn't do this again, would you, if you had another chance?"

He cried: "No! No!"

But he had worked himself into such a state that it took a long time to get him quiet again.

Another man, who had been a showman, had put a bullet through his ankle. When he went before a board, they asked him if he would promise not to do that sort of thing again. He told us he had said: "No, but I make you a promise that next time I'll put it through my nut!"

One man—there were many such cases—had cut his throat. It had been stitched up and had left a hideous scar. He used to look at himself in the glass of one of the windows and wail: "How can I go home with this? How can I look my mother in the face again!"

Tired of this endless lamentation, a Scot in the ward said to him: "Oh, dry up."

"But what can I say to my mother?"

"Tell her," said the Scotty, "that a German did it with his bayonet."

I wondered whether, if he ever did get home to his mother, which I doubted, he would give the suggested explanation. It is difficult to know how to act towards men who give way as completely as these men did. It becomes exceedingly irritating, especially for men whose own nerves are in a weak condition, to have to listen to them. One should have sympathy with them, for they were not to blame for the condition they were in.

The doctor's patience with them was unwearying and he seemed to be able, for the time at least, to take their minds off their woes. He spent a large part of each day in the hospital and it was, probably in consequence, well run and the patients well treated. Only on one or two occasions while I was there did the orderlies use force to subdue a patient. This fact says a great deal for the efficiency and humanity of the management and staff, for it must be borne in mind that a large percentage of the patients, being nerve cases, were by no means easily managed.

But no matter how well such a hospital is managed it cannot be anything but a place of wretchedness and depression. We had nothing to do and couldn't have done anything if it had been there to do. We *couldn't* read. I would look down a page and my eyes would take in the words, but my brain could not take in their meaning. When we were well enough to get up, we walked in the corridor at the end of the ward and talked, and those of us who could played cards. One day, near the end of my time there, the doctor came through and spoke to us. He asked us how we were getting on, if we were happy.

"Happy!" said one of the men. "Who could be happy in this place?"

"I don't see why you should say that," said the doctor. "We are doing our best for you. Is there anything you'd like to have?"

"We'd like a walk," I said. "Could we go for one?"

He was, I could see, rather taken aback, but he did not want to refuse us. "A walk! A good idea! Who wants to go?" and he picked out those who wanted to go and were fit enough. Later on, we came along to the entrance in a state of excitement. We found as many orderlies detailed for the walk as patients. Consequently, the whole thing fell flat. We had hoped to wander about the town by ourselves. We had not wanted this constitutional under escort. However, there was nothing else for it. We went out on the cliffs between Boulogne and Wimereux overlooking the sea. It was pleasant enough there, but we soon got so tired that we were thankful to get back to the hospital. The doctor came for me.

"You're to go before the Board," he said. "Now, you have nothing whatever to worry about. They have heard all about you from me; they only want to ask you a few questions."

I had faced worse things than boards without a tremor,

but I found now,* to my intense annoyance, that I was trembling uncontrollably and the perspiration was running off my hands. My voice, which I tried vainly to render normal, was still the same hollow whisper. I was angry with myself for my inability to control my weakness, and I transferred my resentment against myself to the Board. I regarded them with a suspicion which I don't think was in the least justified. I tried to keep my end up and offset my trembling, which I was afraid they would notice, by being unnecessarily aggressive, thereby, no doubt, increasing the bad impression I had already made. They asked me how I would like to be sent back to the trenches. I answered that they could do what they liked with me, that it was a matter of absolute indifference to me where I was sent.

"Oh come now," they said. "Wouldn't you like us to send you over to England for a spell?"

"I don't care in the least where you send me."

The hospital doctor cut in: "Of course he would like to. He'll be all right when he's had a good rest over there."

Finally he said they had better let me go and he would explain things to me afterwards. As I went out, I heard one of them say: "Of course we don't know how the New Zealand authorities are going to act towards him. We must safeguard him against them."

I got back to the ward, greatly relieved that the ordeal was over, but very dissatisfied with my own behavior. However, it was true that at that time I really didn't care what they did with me.

I think it was the following day that the M.O. took me into his room for a private talk.

"We have fixed up your papers," he said, "for a full pension. You can claim it from the New Zealand government and they'll have to give it to you."

*April 24.

"I wouldn't think of claiming a pension," I said.

"Look on it as compensation. They put you into the army and they are responsible for what has happened to you."

"All the same, I couldn't think of taking it."

"Your people might look on it differently if you don't recover and were to become a burden on them."

"They would look on it just the same way as I would."

"Well, however you feel about it," he said, "we have felt it our duty to make you aware of your legal position* and to protect you as far as we can."

He told me I would soon be leaving the hospital. I was being sent to England, to a place where I could rest in pleasant surroundings. They had tried, he said, to keep me out of the hands of the New Zealand authorities but sooner or later I would have to go back into their hands. "And, judging by their actions towards you and the lengths they went to to compel your submission, I think it is quite likely that they will try to make you give in on some technical point. What will you do in that case?"

"I'll fight them on it."

"Now that's what I wanted to talk to you about," he said. "I am worried about you. Baxter, you must realize that you are past fighting."

He took an interest in me, he continued, and he wanted to impress upon me, for my own sake, that if I tried to fight on anything I would land back in the same condition as when I came into the hospital. I had won all I needed to trouble about. They could not make me serve. Why, then, spoil my chances of recovery? I might think just now that I could do these things, but it would be a long time before I would be able to stand any strain. In six months time I would probably

---

*In regard to his status in the army. If he was a "soldier," his relatives would be entitled to a pension. Again, Baxter repudiates this: the whole point of his stance is that he is not a soldier.

realize much better than I did now what my condition had been and still was. He told me a good deal of what my reactions would be as I passed through various stages on the road to recovery, and he proved to be correct in all he said. I know I owe him a great deal. I don't know what would have become of me if I had not happened to fall into his hands at that time. I don't even know his name, for I never heard it.

Before I left the hospital I was weighed and saw that I was a few ounces over eight stone.* I wondered what I had been when I came. I must have put on some weight in those five weeks. Though still very thin, I was no longer the skeleton I had been. My usual weight, before my arrest, was eleven stone seven.†

---

*112 lbs.
†161 lbs.

10

WHEN WE CAME to Dover, there was great bustle and excitement on shore. We saw the battered hull of the *Vindictive* as we came in. She had been in action at Zeebrugge the night before, and I heard afterwards that she was taken back that night and sunk in the entrance channel. Men were being taken ashore in stretchers, many cases of shellshock.

We were put on a train and told we were going to Southampton. It was a long journey round the coast, and by the time we arrived at the hospital, we were all worn out. We were in a building at some distance from the main hospital. It seemed to be run as a sort of convalescent home. Tired as we were, our spirits rose at the sight of the pleasant surroundings and the sense of freedom that seemed to pervade the place. There were no wards. We slept in bedrooms, two in each. The next day confirmed the favorable impression. The building was no larger than an ordinary house and there only seemed to be about a dozen patients in it altogether. We wandered about the grounds and the adjoining park without restraint. We mixed with the people outside and in the evenings could sit and watch them playing cricket on the green.

One of the orderlies asked me if I were interested in gardens. I said I was. He took me down and introduced me to the gardener, and I spent hours with him, watching him at his work. He was always in good humor and never in a hurry and took a real interest in all he did. I asked him to show me where he got the special soil for his plants, and he took me out into the wood that bordered the garden.

In a day or two, although we had arrived in a state of exhaustion, we began to feel the benefit of the air and the freedom. Appetite stirred in us and energy began to revive. I think now that the M.O. at Wimereux had meant us to remain there. But there was no such luck in store for us.

We had been there a few days when, one morning, an army doctor came strutting in. We, the men who had come from Wimereux, were standing at ease.

"Line them up against the wall," he said to the orderlies. They did so.

"Had any trouble with them?" he asked.

"Oh no, sir, none at all."

He addressed not one word to us, but proceeded to discuss us with the orderlies as if we had been cattle—and very inferior cattle at that. Never having met anything of the kind before, we were all nervous, and when he suddenly seized the eyelid of the first in the row, the man jerked his head back in alarm. The M.O. now condescended to say: "I won't hurt you. I want to look at your eye," and, returning to the attack, regained his hold of the eyelid and pulled it up. The examination was over in a fraction of a second.

"Do you know what day of the week it is?" he asked the man. He didn't know it. "Stand aside."

We had all turned our heads to look. "Keep your face straight," he snapped at me and jerked my eyelid up. "Do you know what time it is?"

I didn't know. We had no watches. There was no clock in

the room and nothing to mark the passage of time for us. But it was noted as a sign of "taking no interest in surroundings." He was the last word in military efficiency and put us all through in less than five minutes. Not one of us could answer the stock questions. Not one of us passed the test. The whole thing was farcical but it had a tragic side for us. We were cast out of that paradise.

A day or two later, we were sent away by train. We asked the orderlies where we were going, but they were vague. To a hospital somewhere near London, they said. On our way we collected another batch of nerve and shellshock cases. Many of these were much worse than we were, but we were all kept together. Some of them were quite without control, crying like children. Every time we passed another train, they would fling themselves screaming onto the floor, tearing at the boards with their teeth and nails. Whereupon the orderlies would fall upon them with their fists and throw them into a corner, where they would be quiet from sheer exhaustion. It may sound brutal to say so, but we felt relief when men were silenced in this fashion. We only just had enough control not to give way ourselves, and when one is just managing to hold on, one can't have much sympathy for those who break down. I felt as if my flesh were being torn off in strips, and it was years before I could see a train come into a station without a sensation of uneasiness.

It was a gloomy journey. We had a feeling of foreboding, and were oppressed with fears of we knew not what. Something vague, shadowy, menacing, lay before us. We had had heavy rainstorms on the journey, but as the train passed through London, the sky cleared. I asked questions of the orderlies and one of them pointed out Westminster Abbey and the Houses of Parliament, as we crossed the Thames.

We arrived at our destination, Bradmore Hospital. By this time most of us were completely knocked up. I have no idea of what happened after our arrival. It is probable that I collapsed from exhaustion, for I remember nothing more until I woke and found myself in bed in a ward. I felt very weak, and it was several days before I could get up. I could see none of the men who had come with me the day before. Most of the men in the ward were sick or wounded. Several of them were dying, and their groans and cries were heart-rending. Two beds beyond me a man was having his wounds dressed. When his body was laid bare it was a ghastly sight that met the eye, for it looked, literally, as though a plowshare had torn it from neck to heel. I was told he had lasted a long time, but had not much further to go. That night his groans grew fainter. He called some names in a familiar way, and all was still.

In the next bed to mine, a bright-faced young chap was sitting up. I spoke with him. He was intelligent and seemed perfectly normal, but before long he poured out a tale of sexual experiences—whether real or imaginary it was impossible to tell—weeping bitterly and imploring me to tell him if there was any forgiveness for him. The next day he had two visitors, women, and he did the same to them. Whether delusions or not, it was a tragedy either way. He was probably quite well fitted to cope with the ordinary demands of life, but the unnatural and extraordinary conditions in which he had found himself had been too much for him, as for so many others.

I was anxious to know what sort of place this was that I had come to. It was not easy to find out while I was in the ward. I raised myself up and looked out of the window. The ward was on the ground floor and there was a large, well-kept lawn outside. A blackbird alighted in the center of it. He raised his tail and balanced himself for a moment, swinging backwards and forwards, and flew off to the nearest trees. They were huge elms in a field not far away. The landscape was green and pleasant and typically English. I sank back again, too tired to keep on looking, but satisfied that things would not be bad when I could get up and leave this ward. Physically, I was comfortable and warm for the first time in months. There were plenty of blankets and my bed was right in front of a pleasant fire.

I was told I could get up. I was to move permanently from that ward and be established in new quarters. Still feeling rather shaky, I was taken along to the M.O.'s room. He started at once, in a very patronizing manner, to question me about my experiences at the Front. He was very anxious to know what conditions were like there, and asked me questions that he would not have ventured to ask anyone else—what sensations did one have in the midst of heavy shellfire?—and others of the same kind. I did not trust him and was not at all inclined to talk about it, so gave him very little satisfaction. He asked me why I had refused orders and I told him briefly what my attitude to war was. He began to hold forth on the law of the survival of the fittest.

Irritation was rising in me and I had difficulty in controlling it. I had heard enough of that stuff, I said. What was happening to the world's best and fittest men? Every day they were being smashed up and slain in the war. He cut me short by asking me suddenly if I would go into the fields to produce food for the people of England. I said I was doing that in New Zealand when the authorities arrested me. It seemed silly to me to leave a farm in New Zealand to go back to nature while I took on planting potatoes in England.

"In any case, I am just out of bed. Would you say I am fit to do farm work?"

"That's not the point," he said. "How much you can do doesn't matter. The point is, will you say that you are willing to do it?"

I was suspicious of this persistence. Why should it matter

to him? It was strongly reminiscent of the way in which officers in Sling and in France had tried to entrap me into doing
something in the army.

"What is my position here?" I asked.

"You are a patient in a military hospital. Now answer my
question. I want a straight answer, yes or no."

"Until I know more about it than I do at the present, my
answer is 'No.'"

He became openly angry and told me that by my stub-
bornness I had put myself into a position of absolute dependence on the army. My anger rose.

"You say I have put myself into a position of dependence
on the army! The New Zealand government and the army
authorities are entirely responsible for what has happened to
me. They knew very well what my attitude was before they
sent me out of New Zealand. I have only stood to my principles, and as for being dependent on the army, let me go out of
here, and I'll find my own way back to New Zealand without
any further help from them."

But he had the last word.

"I'll give you three days in bed for insolence. Orderly, three
days in bed for this man, for insolence." The orderly marched
me off to the bed I had left that day, expecting never to return
to it. I was shaking with excitement and helpless anger. I was
not sorry to be back in bed, but furious that any man should
have it in his power to inflict this humiliation on me and
treat me as if I had been a badly behaved child. I was angry
with myself, too, for having allowed my irritation to get the
better of me, and having, consequently, made such a bad
showing. Anyone in the condition I was in is at a great disadvantage in argument, being so easily roused to excitement.

When I opened my eyes in the morning, I found that a
new patient had come in. He was lying in a bed not far from
me, rolling his eyes and looking round the room. No one

took any notice of him. His eyes lighted on me and he smiled. I spoke to him and he smiled still more. He had dark eyes, straight black hair, and a broad, swarthy face. He was, I learned, a half-caste Maori, which meant that he had a white ancestor some way back. He was a throwback almost entirely to the dark race, only the yellowish tinge of his skin showing that he was not a pure Maori.

When I had finished my three days, I was shifted to a large ward upstairs. It had two long rows of beds and windows along each side which let in plenty of light. On the opposite side of the landing a door opened into a large dining hall. There were about fifty men in the ward, amongst them ten or a dozen New Zealanders. Here I found several of the men who had come with me from Boulogne. Where the others had gone, I don't know. It did not take me very long, once I was out of bed, to find out what sort of place we had come to. It was a prison in every sense of the word. In some ways it was worse than any prison. The men were more utterly helpless in the hands of the orderlies than ever were prisoners in the hands of warders. In that place force and fear reigned triumphant. There was no consideration for the men's nerves, no tact, no persuasion, only threats and force. Did a man offer resistance or give trouble—trouble that often could have been avoided by the exercise of a little tact on the part of the orderly—he would immediately be surrounded by orderlies, and one of them would fell him. They would keep him on the broad of his back, holding down his arms and legs. Sitting on his chest and opening the fastenings at his neck so that he could breathe, they'd ask him if he had had enough. If he said "No," or was silent, one of them knelt on his head and crushed it down on the floor. This left no marks and at the same time never failed to bring about the submission of the patient, who was nearly always weak physically as well as in his nerves, and had no resistance in him. When he had said "that's done it" or "I give in," they let him up and marched him off to the M.O., who sent him into No. VII Ward for a longer or shorter time as the case might be, and sometimes never to return. It must not be imagined that the orderlies were particularly brutal. They were not. But the hospital was run on a system of force and utter disregard for the rights or needs of the patients—a system that gives less trouble than another way—and, that being so, the orderlies used these methods.

There must have been a large number of men in No. VII Ward, and as far as we could observe, they were all completely insane. When we were out on exercise there was only a fence between them and us, and we had plenty of opportunity of seeing and hearing what they were like. I never heard an intelligent word from them, not even a request for tobacco, and yet the babble of their voices rose like an orgy of the damned. With troubled eyes and twisted faces they walked, each man alone. Though there were so many, no two ever walked together. The bonds that unite men had snapped and each man was alone, dreadfully alone. Their lips moved continually, but they could not speak. They could whisper and mutter. They could shout and howl. They had once been men. They had been soldiers who went out to fight. Now they were only human wastage. Alive, and yet life held nothing more for them—only torment. Looking at them I wished that all the world could see these men, could look into their minds and souls, scorched and blasted by the fire blight of war, and hear them cry for a loss—the greatest loss of all— which they feel, but cannot comprehend.

Having this horror before their eyes, the threat of being sent into No. VII kept the men in our ward in a state of abject terror. It was no idle threat, they knew, and against the sentence there was no appeal. It was looked upon as a death sentence, for they knew that the effect of putting in there—a man whose nerves were already weak—was often to drive him insane.

The majority of the men on our side of the barrier were perfectly sane and rational at all times, but most of them suffered from frightful fits of depression. Their nerves were bad and the atmosphere of the place was depressing to the last degree. Of treatment there was absolutely none. We never saw the M.O., except when some unfortunate was brought before him to be dumped into No. VII. The orderlies looked upon us as only one degree better than the men on the other side of the barrier, and treated us accordingly.

The following episode will convey an idea of their attitude towards us. At meals the Tommies sat at a long table running down one side of the hall. The New Zealanders sat at a smaller table by themselves. One morning at breakfast, a day or two after I had been shifted into the upstairs ward, we were all served the usual plate of porridge, but no spoons were supplied.

Someone called out: "We've got no spoons!"

An orderly shouted back: "You can go ahead. You're not getting any!"

Some of the Tommies began to eat, but there were stifled curses from others. One of the New Zealanders asked: "What are we going to do?"

I rose from the table: "We are going to get spoons, but don't let anyone touch a mouthful of that porridge 'til I come back."

I walked up to the orderlies' counter. Two New Zealanders followed me. I said to the orderly: "Will you give me a spoon, please?"

"We are not issuing spoons," he rapped out.

"So I see," said I, "but the New Zealanders won't eat without spoons—don't imagine it."

He looked at our table where the strike was holding good.

Reluctantly, he handed me a spoon. Then all the other New Zealanders walked up and got spoons. One Tommy came up and demanded one, too, but he hadn't enough support. He was told his mates were all eating without spoons, and he could go and do likewise. They all submitted, and from that time had to lap their porridge as best they could from their plates. It was sickening to have to see and hear them at it. When one took into account the atmosphere they lived in, one could not blame them, though I do think that if they had stood together they would have won. At the same time I must admit that my revolt was mainly bluff and had very little behind it. If the orderlies had continued to refuse us spoons, we could have done nothing and would have had to lap our porridge like the rest.

The rationing was so short that we were in a state of continual hunger. The principal diet was porridge and potatoes. Of meat we got so little that it was no more than the taste of it in our mouths when we did have it. We got potatoes and sometimes a small portion of cabbage or other vegetable for dinner, one potato if they were a fair size and two if they were small. Jackets and grape marks and grubs were all devoured. No food was ever left over or anything that had the taste of food. Of bread—bitter, sodden stuff, made from potatoes and some kind of dark meal—we got very little indeed. We usually had a small allowance of cheese for tea, a very small quantity of bread with a little fat on it, and a cup of thin, watery cocoa. Sometimes, in addition, we got some biscuits. For breakfast we had the cocoa again and porridge. The quality of the food, except for the bread, was all right. It was the quantity that fell so far short of what was needed. In many cases the condition of the men's nerves was due to their physical state, and nourishing food—and plenty of it—would have made all the difference. We were told that everyone in England was short of food, but that they were as short as we were I don't believe. The orderlies had plenty. At the other hospital the food had been of good quality and sufficient, and my brothers, who were both in hospital in England, told me that the food was ample. But these were ordinary hospitals, for ordinary men. We were different. We didn't matter and nothing we said would be listened to. We were kept alive and kept secure and that was all.

We were allowed out for exercise in the morning and again in the afternoon. We walked up and down in front of the building, between points where orderlies stood on guard. Inside or outside, we were never for one moment away from their watching eyes. Once, to test the strictness of their watch, I slipped behind some bushes where I could see all that went on. It was only a matter of seconds before one of the watching orderlies missed me, and his eyes moved round in search of me. In no time he had spotted me and signed to me to come out. Another time I was digging up dandelion roots with a piece of stick. They were juicy and they eased my hungry stomach a little. Glancing over my shoulder, I saw two orderlies stalking me. They sprang on me.

"Trying to poison yourself! We've been watching you."

It took me a long time to convince them that dandelion roots are not poisonous.

We had tea at five o'clock and went to bed for the night immediately afterwards, although there were still hours of daylight. We were not allowed to get up again for any reason whatever. Though the latrines were just across the landing we were not allowed to go to them, because in that case the orderly on night duty would have to leave the ward unwatched while he supervised in the latrines. Hence there had to be a chamber-pot under every bed. There were about fifty of them and every day a patient would be told off by the orderlies to clean them, bring them to a state of shining perfection, and stack them up for inspection. The job was hated.

There was more trouble over it than over any other. Only certain patients had to take it in turn while the others were exempt. What this discrimination was based on we never knew. It was submitted to, perforce. The will of the orderlies was law. I passed through one morning and saw the Maori patient, Fred Parsons, who had lately come into our ward, just finishing the job for the second time, having failed to pass the inspector-orderly with them on his first attempt.

He called out to me as I passed: "Do you think this will do?"

He had built them into a beautiful pyramidal structure, but just as he was putting the finishing touch to it, there was a crash, and down it came. An orderly came up, shouting: "What's this? What's this?" Fred's nerves were already on edge with having to do twice over a job he loathed, and the crash had further upset him. The orderly's shouts were the last straw. He still had a pot in his hand, and, swinging it in the air, sent it hurtling into the pile. Orderlies swarmed like bees. Fred gave one wild glance round. Then, filled with the primitive instinct to escape at any cost, he fled into a little room at the end of the ward and made for the open window. He was caught by the legs before he could get through, and it ended in his being marched off to the M.O. He appeared among us again in the evening, as meek as a lamb. Next day, he told me all about it.

"You'll go to No. VII and you'll stay in there until you learn to behave yourself," said the M.O., "and you'd better make up your mind to do it quickly, for I won't come at once when you send for me."

"I won't send for you," said Fred, still defiant and not realizing what he was in for.

But he had not been long in No. VII before his pride broke down utterly, and he was humbly and abjectly imploring the orderlies to get the doctor for him. It was the end of the day before his frantic appeals were listened to and he was allowed out.

"A dreadful place," said Fred. "Not a man there I could make friends with."

Everything about the place was kept spotlessly clean. The floors were of wood, kept in a high state of polish. Such a standard was not required of the bodies of the patients, but we were kept reasonably clean. For the first few weeks after we were admitted, we had a bath every week. After that we had a shower, also weekly. During the bathing stage the patients were soaped, washed, and dried by the orderlies, although, as a rule, quite capable of doing it for themselves. The first time I had a bath at Bradmore, one orderly washed me while another with a notebook looked for marks, boils, scabies, or any other manifestation of skin trouble, writing down what he found, and on subsequent occasions checking up any alterations. He was scrutinizing me carefully from the back.

"What on earth are you doing?" I asked.

"I'm looking for your wound. Is this it?"

"What are you talking about?" I exclaimed in annoyance. "I've got no wound."

"Yes, you have. You've got a wound stripe on your coat."

"Then it's a mistake and it'll have to come off."

I couldn't convince him. As a parting shot he remarked in triumph: "You've got a wound all right. It's in your papers!"

When I afterwards got my coat back, I looked to see if he had spoken the truth about the stripe. Sure enough, it was there! It seemed strange that I hadn't noticed it, coming to Bradmore. Having no knife to cut it off with, I chewed and tore it with my teeth until I got it off.

There was no recreation of any kind. At Wimereux there had been cards for those who were well enough to play. Here there were none. No books, no magazines, no papers. Only a little publication called *The New Zealander*, which gave lists of men in hospitals and occasional items of news from New Zealand. Most of us were by that time capable of reading, if only for a little, and something very light. But there was nothing. No services were ever held. No ministers of religion came near us. Outside we wandered aimlessly within our narrow prescribed limits. In the ward we sat or stood about. We could smoke. The hospital allowance to smokers was twenty cigarettes a week. No matches were allowed, but every morning an orderly came in with one in his hand. "Here, you men, light up." One man got a light from him and that served for the whole ward, each man giving a light to his neighbor. One match, one ward, very economical. Afterwards, there was generally someone smoking from whom one could get a light.

We only had one another's company, and the large majority were gloomy, depressed, and utterly crushed by the position in which they found themselves and the frightful atmosphere of the place. Many of them had turns in which they would sit for hours, gazing before them with an expression of fixed and hopeless misery. Once or twice while I was there, there were attempts at suicide in our ward. One man stood up suddenly at breakfast and cut his throat with a knife that he had managed to secrete, carefully watched as we were. In less time than it takes to tell, the surgeon was on the spot. The man's veins were clipped up and he was taken away, to be stitched at their leisure. Whether he lived or died we never heard. He never came back to us. This may seem to imply the necessity for precautions, but the large majority of the men were not suicidal, and in better surroundings and in an entirely different atmosphere would these attempts at suicide have been made? If we could have gone outside and mingled with other people as we had done at the other hospital, what a difference that would have made!

Fred Parsons, whom we nicknamed Rua,[*] provided the sole enlivenment to the general gloom. Underneath it all he was bitter and realized his position as acutely as any of us. His pride encouraged him to give full rein to his natural humor. Being a Maori, he got away with things that would have landed any of us into trouble. It pleased him to regard the place as a zoo and when he saw people coming in he would call out: "Roll up, roll up and see the animals! They are all quite docile and will eat out of your hand and glad to get the chance!"

As we came up the concrete steps from exercise outside, the orderlies shouted at us to look sharp about it and hurry up. Fred turned round and shouted to us: "Come on, Bradmore heroes, over the top!"

He gave us a speech on the Maori. He held forth on the wrongs of the Maori race. Their country, their lands that they had held for centuries, had been taken from them by the Europeans. He forgot his own drop of European blood and identified himself with his dark ancestors.

After he had finished he came over to me. "How did I do? All right?"

"What about the Moriaris,[†] Fred?" I asked.

He grinned. "They killed everyone. Glad you didn't say that when I was talking. I couldn't have said a word."

Once or twice we had visits of inspection from army officers. We were lined up and they inspected us, asked a

---

[*] Refers to Rua Kenana, a Maori prophet with many Tuhoe people followers. In 1908 he established a community at Maungapohatu in the Urewera Mountains which rejected white presence while retaining some of their administrative structures. During the war, he followed a pacifist line and discouraged volunteering while saying those who wanted to could join. Eventually, he was regarded as working in league with the Kaiser along with causing trouble over land. Various charges were laid against him and in April 1916, police converged on Maungapohatu: two Maori were killed and four police wounded. Rua and five others were arrested. Rua was sentenced to one year hard labor and with an additional eighteen months imprisonment. There was much resistance by the Maori.

[†] An early race that lived in New Zealand alongside the Maori.

question here and there, and that was the end of it. Fred's broad, cheerful face stood out in contrast to the general appearance of despondency.

One officer was moved to address him: "Well, my man, and what's your trouble?"

"Feeblemindedness, sir," said Fred, promptly, with a perfectly unmoved face. ("Poor fellow, he must be pretty far gone to admit it like that.")

"Oh, and how does it show itself?"

"In coming to this bloody war, sir."

The officer gave a snort and turned away. Many of us would have liked to have emulated Fred when we were asked patronizing questions, but we were not game to. We knew we would not have got away with it as he did.

For the New Zealanders, there was just one green spot in the desert. Every week we were visited by Mrs. Archer. She distributed cigarettes, inquired after the health of each man, and endeavored, without much success, to elicit something more than the usual "Thank you" and "Better, thank you," which was our limit. The consciousness of the way in which we were regarded made us tongue-tied and stiff, and I don't suppose Mrs. Archer had any idea of the eagerness with which we looked forward to that visit and counted the days until it came round again. It was the one break in the monotony of our existence, the one contact with the outer world, and took us out of the dreary round of our own companionship.

There was one man who tried to make up for our shyness, on one occasion at least, by being over-bold. When we were admitted into the narrow, passage-like room in which the visits took place, he was in the lead. He went straight up to Mrs. Archer and kissed her. We were very angry. It made us look a lot of fools, for she would certainly regard us as being in the same category with him, capable of any crazy action.

In the weekly publication I have mentioned, there appeared a report of the condition of all the New Zealanders in hospitals. Every week there was a rush for the new number to see what was said about us, and every week, with monotonous regularity, there appeared opposite each of the names of the New Zealanders at Bradmore the remark: "Much about the same." The reports were supposed to be sent in by the official visitors. There was much speculation as to who was responsible for them in our case. As we never saw the M.O., we judged that the orderlies must supply Mrs. Archer with a report on our condition. We always looked anxiously for clues as to how we were supposed to be getting on, and as to whether we were likely to be getting out in any definite time. As far as we knew, our fate lay in the hands of the orderlies, but what it was, we had no means of knowing.

I said to some of the others that I thought, considering how much we appreciated Mrs. Archer's visits, that we should try to express our gratitude to her in some way. They all agreed that it should be done, but no one seemed ready to do it. We were held back by the knowledge of how we were looked upon. Victims of a heartless and brainless system, we reacted naturally to it, were judged by our reactions, and the verdict was against us. I determined, however, to put it all out of my mind for the moment, and, the next time Mrs. Archer came, to speak to her in an ordinary way. She had a small boy with her. I made some remark about him. She responded at once and we talked about him; her grandson she said he was. I told her how greatly we appreciated her visits, that she must not think, because we had not said anything about it, that we were not grateful to her for her kindness. For once a polite speech was absolutely sincere, for everything I said was true. She asked me if I had written home. I hadn't, I said. I hadn't felt able to. She offered to write for me. I knew that my people would be much more alarmed at hearing from someone else about me than they would be at not hearing from me at all, and I thought it would be better to wait until I could write myself. As a matter of fact, I only wrote one letter while I was in Bradmore and that was in reply to my brother Sandy, who was in hospital in England with rheumatic fever and who had seen my name in the lists. I found it impossible to write.

When *The New Zealander* appeared the next week following my conversation with Mrs. Archer, the other patients were still "much about the same" but A. McC. Baxter was "very much improved." There was now no doubt as to who was responsible for the reports. Fred Parsons brought me the paper in a great state of excitement. "How wonderful, and all in one week," I said, laughing. Fred was a little upset. He was inclined to believe the printed word and doubted me when I explained that I hadn't really improved any more than he had, and that all anyone needed to do was to put up a little sensible conversation.

"Well," he said, "if that's it, don't do it again, or you'll be going off and leaving us, 'much about the same.'"

Another time he brought me the publication, which sometimes had items of interest to New Zealanders. He showed me a heading: "Last member of notorious Baxter family sent to jail."

"Any relation of yours?" he inquired.

"Yes, that's my brother."

He was amused.

We were told that the New Zealanders had been invited out to dinner by an estate owner in the neighborhood. I refused to go. I gave the others as my reason that he wouldn't want me if he knew what I was and I didn't want to accept hospitality on false pretenses. But my real reason, which I did not want to give, was that I did not want to be entertained as one of the Bradmore patients and all that that implied. The others went. They said, on their return, that I should have gone, that the host had taken them round and shown them his prize cattle, which I, being a farmer, would have been so much better able to appreciate. But I found out afterwards that most of them had not really enjoyed it, and for the same reason that had prevented me from going.

Not long after this an orderly whom I did not know—I think he was from some other part of the hospital—told me he was having a day off in London and was allowed to take anyone he liked with him.

"And I've chosen you," he said.

I was a little surprised as I had never to my knowledge, seen him before. However, I said I would like to go, but that I had no money.

"That doesn't matter," he said. "I'll see to it. It won't be much, anyway."

"But do you think I'll be allowed to go, just with you?"

"That's all fixed up," he assured me.

So there was nothing more to bother about, and we went to London, taking a bus and then a train.

We went up and down escalators and traveled what seemed vast distances by tube. We had a cup of tea and a bun somewhere for twopence. I found the rush and roar of the traffic a positive nightmare. The speed of everything terrified me and I was at the point of breaking down.

Trying hard to keep my control, I said: "Let's go somewhere out of all this rush and noise."

My companion was quite ready to. He took me to quieter back streets and to see second-hand shops which seemed to interest him. Afterwards he took me to the only sights he thought worth showing me: a monument to the *Titanic*, made out of wreckage, and a dog that had saved forty lives, but was now stuffed and used as a collecting-box. At frequent intervals he would say: "Wait for me a moment," and disappear. In

WE SHALL NOT CEASE

a few minutes, he would reappear, sometimes from the opposite direction. These actions of his puzzled me a good deal. I now, of course, realize that the whole expedition was a rare instance of the use of tact on the part of the hospital management, and was taken with the sole object of noting my reactions to outside life. The disappearances of my escort were, of course, to ascertain how I would behave when left to myself. No doubt he had me spotted all the time and would have caught me at once if I had attempted to abscond. The scheme was entirely successful as far as I was concerned, for, strange to say, I never suspected it and remained to the end under the impression that the expedition was a spontaneous act of kindness on the part of the orderly. The visit to the neighboring estate owner had been intended, of course, as a test of the same kind.

Not long after this, a New Zealand colonel walked in one day while we were out on exercise. The New Zealanders were all collected up on the lawn, and he told us we were being sent back to New Zealand. I felt dull and apathetic and took very little notice. It all seemed dim and vague and far away. The others, I know, felt the same, for there was no sign of excitement or enthusiasm. This may seem strange; but for a long time we had been so utterly crushed that our feelings had become deadened. Just as if half-a-dozen men were drawn at random from any of the clinks or compounds I was in, it would be found that the average of intellect would be much higher than in the same number drawn from the army at large, so the men I was with at Bradmore were, almost without exception, of particularly fine temperament.

To my surprise the colonel called me out.

He shook me warmly by the hand and, turning aside with me, he said: "I want to speak to you for a moment. I know all about your history and I am surprised to find you so well. I know you have had objections to war and I know something of what you have suffered. I don't want to ask any questions. I only want to assure you that you have my very best wishes. I hope you soon get back to your own people and make a speedy recovery."

I stood there speechless. Perhaps I murmured: "Thanks."

I was completely bowled over and couldn't trust myself to say anything. It takes time to get used to being treated as a human being, just as it takes time to become accustomed to harsh treatment.

11

WE TRAVELED DOWN to Southampton by train. As we walked up the gangway of the boat that was to take us across the Channel, a New Zealander whom I did not know told me to follow him. He took me to some place where there was a bed, and at that time there was no one else there. I was so tired that I could hardly take in the objects about me, and I was only clear on one thing—that here was a place to lie down.

"You're tired," he remarked. "You can lie down there whenever you like, but wait a bit 'til I bring you a cup of tea."

He returned in a minute or two with a mug of tea and a slice of white bread and butter. I took a mouthful of the tea and a bite of the bread. I thought I had never tasted anything like it in my life. The bread seemed to melt in my mouth. I finished it and lay down and in a moment I was asleep. When I opened my eyes it was morning, and the boat was still.

"Haven't we started yet?" I asked the others in surprise.

"What are you thinking about?" they said. "We're at Le Havre."

We were put on board a train and for five days we traveled slowly through France. We passed the outskirts of Paris. For a long time—it seemed for a day or two—we traveled down the valley of the Rhone. For most of the time we lay stretched out on the seats, too tired to care what was passing by outside. When we arrived at Marseille the *Marama* was lying at the wharf and I saw "Dunedin" written across her stern with the same indifference with which I had heard the news of our projected journey. Instead of embarking at once, we went up to a camp close to the town, where tents were pitched for us. There we remained for several days, under the shade of high, spreading trees. The hills beyond the town looked so inviting that I hoped to reach them when I had recovered a little from my weariness, and thought I could do so quite easily. An opportunity presented itself. A mental patient had got away and volunteers had been called to look for him.

"Say we'll look for him," I said to the men with me. "We don't need to really, but it will give us a chance to make for those hills."

No one seemed to think it surprising that we should hunt for a mental patient. We were only told that we must not be away for more than an hour. We set out cheerfully, but the hills receded as we advanced and we soon realized that we had neither the strength nor the time to get anywhere near them. The missing man was located a few hundred yards from the camp, eating fruit in a peasant's garden.

Our time in camp was up and we went on board the *Marama*. A man was standing at the top of the gangway, taking our names as we came up. When I gave mine, he looked at me sharply.

"Are you one of the Baxters?" he inquired. "One of the deported men?"

I said I was.

"I can't talk to you just now," he said, "but I'll see you later."

He came to me on the deck afterwards and told me,

among other things, that there had been a stir in New Zealand about the deported men. He wanted to know if I knew anything about the others, but I could tell him very little. He turned out to be the barber, and as I was not allowed a razor I had plenty of opportunities for conversation with him.

The first time I went to him for a shave I said: "The authorities are looking after me very carefully. I am not allowed a razor for fear I should cut my own or someone's throat, and yet the sea is there and nothing to stop me jumping into it."

The barber, smiling nervously, agreed with everything I said. Later, he came to know me better and ceased to be nervous.

We appeared before the doctor in charge of our ward and four of us were ordered to drink stout. Several of the men considered they should have had it too, and when I found that it disagreed with me, one of them suggested that I should go on getting my bottle and let him have it. But the next time I went up for it, a glass was poured out for me and I was told to drink it then and there, to the annoyance of the disappointed candidate. I told the doctor it didn't agree with me. He told me to persevere with it, and I did for a while, but as it never ceased to disagree, I finally gave it up as I didn't think it would be doing me any good.

We sailed through the Mediterranean under the orders of a Spanish officer who took his directions from the Germans.[*] At night we were brilliantly lit up and had a ring of green lights round the bulwarks. The skies were a stainless blue and a light breeze made the silver sea ripple and dance in the sunlight. We passed between Corsica and the mainland. So I had seen where the great Corsican was born and where he had died.

This was all very pleasant. The Bradmore men were

---

[*]Here, Baxter is joking: The boat was so lit up that any German U-boat could see it.

beginning to cheer up considerably and every day were finding more interest in life. Except in the matter of razors, we were treated just like the other men and we had begun to make new friends and acquaintances among them. One day one of the men came up to me. He was a friendly, intelligent chap, but he had been very much crushed by the months he had spent in Bradmore.

He said: "They've done for us all, absolutely!"

I looked at him. His face was gray. "What's happened?" I asked.

"Come and I'll show you."

I followed him to where a list of patients' names had been posted up, with the man's complaint appended to each name. The Bradmore patients and several others who had come from hospitals of the same kind had "mental" written against their names.

"Look at that," said the man with me. "I've made lots of friends since I've been on board and now what'll they think of me? Mental!"

It is this total disregard of their feelings that makes it difficult for men to recover. There was one exception on the list. My name appeared without anything whatever opposite it. Simply the name and nothing more.

There were other patients on board from mental hospitals, beside the Bradmore men. One of these men had had frightful experiences in a military prison. One day on deck he was talking of the cruelty and brutality he had seen and experienced there, and quite a crowd had gathered up to listen to him. He was a quiet and gentle sort of man, but at the same time one could see that he was determined. He told us that he had been put into a cell with human excrement in a corner. He had asked to have it removed or to be allowed to remove it himself. For answer the warders rubbed his face in it. They kept him in that cell for days without letting him out at all, or allowing him any means of attending to his needs. The previous occupant had evidently been treated in the same way. He told his story quietly and without excitement. Only when he came to the part about himself, his face showed that it was difficult for him to tell it.

While he was talking, an officer had come up and overheard part of this. "That's a lot of nonsense that you're telling," he said. "There isn't a word of truth in it."

Almost immediately afterwards the man was put in the padded cell. This was out on the deck in full sight of everyone, and whenever it had an occupant, he could be plainly seen through the open observation hole, so that everyone knew who had been put in there.

I went up to it and spoke to him, amid warnings from the other men of: "Don't you go, or they'll put you in there, too."

"I understand," he said to me. "Not another word do I say. They've got me all right."

And they had. Putting him in the padded cell had the effect, as it was intended to, of making the other men doubt everything he had said. Only those who were listed as coming from mental hospitals would be put there, and during the voyage several of them were. I saw Fred Parsons there once. I asked him what was the matter, but he either didn't know or didn't care to say. It was a wonderful institution, that padded cell. It could work miracles. I never heard of the men who were put in there being violent, but after they had been in there a day or two they could be given perfect liberty on board and were meek for the rest of the voyage. We were like the habitual criminal under the Dog Act. Other men might argue and quarrel and fight, but we had to be very careful. I was talking on deck to a group of men on war and conscription. An officer, not satisfied with the good hearing I was getting, came up and challenged what I was saying. I had said that a large proportion of soldiers on all fronts were fighting because they were compelled to, and would be glad to cease firing any time they had the chance. I asked him what would happen if, in all the armies on the Western Front, the death penalty and all other punishments were taken off.

"You must have these things," he said. "You can't have discipline without them."

"You can't have war without discipline, and discipline means 'kill or be killed.' Isn't that forcing men to fight?"

I felt at a disadvantage having to be so controlled and careful in order to give them no excuse for putting me in the padded cell.

There was a man on board who had been with us at Bradmore. His one trouble was that, when summoned before an officer or placed in any position that made him nervous, he would give a hop on one leg, just one hop. We told him that he must not do it, that he must control himself, especially before officers, or it would bring him into trouble. He said he would be careful, but when he was again before an officer the same thing happened. He listened respectfully and answered in the right place. Then, just as he turned away, he gave that little skip. It was his downfall. When we disembarked, he was detained and sent to hospital.

The voyage passed quickly. Having neither cargo nor passengers to take on at ports, we didn't take the usual time that passenger steamers do to make the voyage. We reached Colombo, the first port at which we were allowed to land. At Port Said no shore leave had been given, though we were there the whole day. One of the padres gave me a pound note and arranged for me to have a trip ashore. I went under escort, but once on shore the escort didn't bother about me any more, and I went round with them as one of them. At Albany I also went on shore and returned with a large bunch of the wildflowers that are at their best in Western Australia in September. They were much appreciated by the nurses.

We arrived at Auckland.* A military doctor came on board and interviewed me. I have never met such bitter hostility as he showed towards me. He told me I was not to imagine I had beaten the military authorities because I had been brought back to New Zealand. It was solely on account of my health that I had been sent back. I would not be able to say that I had won in the stand I had taken against military service.

"If you attempt to, you'll find that you won't be allowed. You're not going to get away with it."

I had to listen to him and was not permitted to say a single word in reply. I don't think I showed any sign that his words had had any effect on me, but inwardly I was not so calm. I had gloomy forebodings, realizing, even then, that circumstances had given the authorities a hold over me which they would probably know how to use.

We went down the east coast to Wellington. Those who were destined for other ports were not, of course, allowed to land. We were not long in when the M.O. in charge of our ward came to me and informed me that the Minister of Defense had come on board and wished to see me. He looked very amused, and when he took me down to the cabin to my visitor—or rather visitors, for there was another man with the Minister—he could hardly keep his face straight long enough to make his introduction. Then he left us. The second man attempted to keep the interview on an ordinary level of politeness by making some inquiries about my health. But his colleague had come on board with one object in view, and he plunged into his questionings without any preliminaries. Was I still of the same mind with regard to military service?

I said I was.

He told me that they had been charged with treating objectors cruelly. Had I been badly treated in the army?

*September 21, 1918.

I said I had received treatment that I would call cruel.

He asked me what I was doing while I was at the Front?

Anything I had done, I said, was done voluntarily as an individual and not under military orders.

"Are you a conscientious objector?"

"I was. . . ," I was beginning, when he broke in: "You were—are you not one now?"

But I had to dash his hopes. "I was called one in the army," I went on, "but I don't call myself by any name."

"Then why do you object to military service?"

"Because I am opposed to war."

"Do you know anything about No. 1 Field Punishment?" he asked next.

"Not much," I answered, hoping he would be satisfied with that and not ask me any more about it.

But he continued. I had written a letter from France which had been published, and in it I had said that I had been subjected to this punishment. Was it true?

I said I didn't know the letter had been published; I hadn't written it for publication; but what I had said in it was quite true.

"Show me how it's done," he demanded.

I stood against the cabin wall and described No. 1 Field Punishment to him to the best of my ability. He afterwards described me in a statement which he published shortly afterwards in the newspapers, as "surly and morose." I answered all his questions politely. I demonstrated my torture to him without a word of protest. What more could he ask? I was not effusive or subservient. *That* I never was, or could be, no matter how crushed I might be. At the conclusion of the interview, he asked me what I intended to do, and I replied that I could not say until I knew what was going to be done with me.

Two women friends came on board to see me. They had

visited me in the barracks and in prison before I left New Zealand. They wanted to have an account of my experiences from me. In my anxiety to prove that I was all right mentally, and in the reaction from the interview immediately before, I am sure I gave them an entirely false impression.

We passed on down to Otago, calling at Lyttelton on the way. When the time came for disembarking, I went up to the office with the rest to get my landing pass. I was given a card with a date on which I was to report at Dunedin Hospital.

"And understand that you are to be there at that time," said the officer to me, "or there will be trouble."

"Yes, I understand," I said. He was not doing this to the other men. "But if I'm feeling quite well or if I find it difficult to come in?" I asked.

"You'll obey orders and report in uniform or you'll be arrested," was the harsh answer, and I felt it bitterly, for I had had some hopes of getting free of it all.

Guards with fixed bayonets lined the wharf. Such a show of force seemed ridiculous to men who had not met that sort of thing, even in France. To show their anger and contempt they leapt the rails and swarmed into the wharf, disregarding bayonets, guards, and gangways.

My people were waiting for me. I think they had expected to find me completely changed and were relieved to find I hadn't altered. As soon as I got home I got out of uniform, anxious to make the adjustment to ordinary life as quickly as possible. I so longed to be free of everything to do with the past two years. People were friendly, though often nervous and not knowing what to say, and what they did say often irritated me intensely. We went out to tea a night or two after I came home.

One of the women present, a relative, asked me: "And you were in France?"

"Yes, I was in France."

"How lovely for you to get a chance to see all those places. I believe France is a very beautiful country."

"Yes, it was lovely for me," I said savagely.

I don't suppose she meant much more than to make polite conversation, but it was not a successful choice of subject, and I longed to do something to make them realize that war wasn't just a pleasant picnic. There seemed to be a wide gulf between me and all the people I knew. It was not because they were unfriendly, but because they all seemed to be just exactly what they had always been. Everything seemed to touch me on the raw. The policeman who had arrested me came to see me about some business. Angry thoughts rose in me at the sight of him. I found that I thought violently, spoke violently, and had difficulty in refraining from acting violently.

The day came when I was supposed to report at the hospital. Very unwillingly I got back into uniform. I thought it best to go in. It was, I hoped, only a preliminary to discharging me, and as above all else I wanted to be free of them, I did not wish to give them any excuse for delaying it. I had to report in the morning. I went in with the morning bus, was told to wait, and hung about the hospital until the afternoon. At last I was allowed to come up and report to the sergeant who was dealing with these cases. He asked me a perfunctory question or two, and gave me a card, telling me to report again on a given date two or three days later.

"What do I report for?" I asked. "Is it for treatment? And what treatment do I get?"

"You've got to report," he said.

"And supposing I don't come in?"

"You'll be brought in. You just remember your position and don't try any nonsense. You can't afford to."

I asked to be allowed to see the doctor and, after waiting a long time, was accorded an interview with him. From this interview I realized beyond any doubt that I was placed in a position in which I could fight no further. When I said I wanted nothing but a chance to earn my living, I was laughed at. I was a patient and my only chance of liberty lay in doing all the authorities wanted. This meant report in uniform, accept the pay they sent me, and be discharged like any other soldier. What the consequences would be if I refused I knew, both from the way they regarded me and from my own condition. The authorities knew well that they had a mighty lever in their hands, and no matter which way I turned they had me in their power. A few days after my arrival in New Zealand, the Minister of Defense had published a statement concerning me, declaring that I was well, did not need to be sent to a hospital of any kind, and could proceed to my home. That gave the impression that I was free, but the fact was that the authorities still held me hard and fast. They could publish what they pleased about me, but in my position I was unable to state my case or make any reply. While it stated I was suffering from no disability, I was compelled to report in uniform at the hospital every few days for many weeks—not for any treatment, for I received none. The object was, as far as I could see, to grind me down and make me realize how completely I was in their power. Seeing no way out, I agreed to do what they required. Even then, the drilling process still went on. I would go in in the morning to report, and would be told to wait. I had to wait there for many hours, sometimes until late afternoon, seeing others who came in long after me attended to before me. This was done deliberately. If I protested, I was treated by the sergeant as a creature without sense or human feeling. People wondered, seeing me going in day after day, always in uniform. I could not explain.

At last, one day when I reported, I was shown into a room with a group of military men at one end of it, some sitting and some standing. The doctor whom I had seen before introduced me. He said they wanted to ask me a few questions if I didn't mind.

I said: "Yes, certainly."

Then I turned and looked at them and every face seemed hostile. I was asked a question or two which I could not answer. They were the usual test questions, and, as I told them with some irritation, proved nothing whatever.

"What are you?" thundered the man who seemed to be the chief among them, probably the chairman.

"A man! What do you take me for?" I replied.

Then a torrent of angry words was let loose on me.

"I didn't come here to be insulted by you!" I shouted, and made for the door.

"Catch him! Catch him!" they roared.

I was seized by the orderlies and dragged back into the room and the door was shut and guarded.

For a time there was nothing but pandemonium. The doctor tried to calm things down and reasoned with me. I said I would not answer a single question unless I was treated with civility. This caused a fresh outbreak. Finally, the doctor managed to arrange that all questions addressed to me should be asked through him. This was agreed to by the board, but it appeared that by that time they were too angry to ask any questions.

The doctor then made a few remarks to me, told me that no one had any right to say anything against my character, and let me go, with the information that I did not need to report any more. And so that scene ended.

It was not until years afterwards that I realized that I had appeared before a Medical Board. It never entered my head that doctors would behave in such a manner. Soon after, I received my discharge. So determined were the authorities to make me out a soldier that it was declared in the discharge that I had served every day that I had been in the army, from the time I was arrested until the time I was discharged, without any ineffective periods. In order to substantiate this, my character had to be given as "good," a note being added to the effect that this was the highest that could be obtained by anyone who had served less than two and a half years. I could now consider myself free.

Not long after, however, I received a notice telling me to report to the police. When I went in, I asked the policeman to whom I reported what this was for. He told me it was just a formality, that every returned soldier had to report. I made inquiries afterwards and found this to be incorrect. Whether it was always done in cases like mine, or whether it was done in my case alone in order to intimidate me, I don't know. The policeman was very decent about it. He went on to say that though he had to send in a report about me at regular intervals, he had other means of finding out and would not require me to come in any more as he saw it worried me.

And so my experiences in the army ended.

Afterword

THE DEFENSE Department, wanting to make examples of the Fourteen, were under the mistaken belief that the objectors, once sent to Europe and subjected to war, would quickly knuckle under. All were eventually broken, one by one, although the Army grossly misjudged the objectors' resolve.

David Gray was transported by mistake as he belonged to a recognized religious sect (those not belonging to a government-recognized religious sect were subject to conscription), and he was allowed to remain at Sling.

At Sling, the first to be subjugated were Frederick Adin, Lewis Penwright, and Albert Sanderson. After 28 days of detention—which consisted of solitary confinement, forced dressing, handcuffs, verbal and physical abuse, and a bread and water diet—they submitted.

On October 6, 1917, the ten remaining men were shipped to France. At Etaples Base they were threatened with being shot, a strategy that broke Daniel Maguire, Thomas Harland, and John Baxter—Baxter being already weak with illness.

Of the rest, Garth Ballantyne, William Little, and Alexander Baxter were sent forward to the lines, court-martialed, and three times threatened with the death penalty. They were sentenced to two years' hard labor and were sent to a prison in Dunkirk. Initially, upon refusing to work, they were put in solitary confinement, and fed a bread and water diet. After agreeing to work, they were still denied hot drinks and underclothing and were worked from 6 a.m. every day despite the weather. Little and Alexander Baxter were eventually hospitalized with bronchitis and Ballantyne with fever. Finally the three agreed to become stretcher-bearers. Little was killed in action.

Besides Archibald Baxter, Mark Briggs, and Lawrence Kerwin, Henry Patton was also subjected to No. 1 field punishment. After 28 days of No. 1 field punishment, Patton, on January 1, 1918, agreed to become a stretcher-bearer. Kerwin, physically weakened, was hospitalized and, upon recovery, became a stretcher-bearer on March 28.

Only Archibald Baxter and Mark Briggs remained defiant until the end: Archibald broken mentally, and Mark Briggs, the uncompromising leader of the Fourteen, broken physically. He was declared "unfit for service."

Long after the war, Archibald Baxter was harassed by the government for his stance. In the 1960s, all references to his punishment were removed from his army file for fear that his son, James, would use them in the campaign against compulsory military training.

Briggs returned to his auctioneering business and from 1936 to 1954 was a legislative councillor. He died in 1965.

Garth Ballantyne, the last survivor of the Fourteen, died in 1984.

Bibliography

Baker, Paul, *King and Country call: New Zealanders, Conscription and the Great War.* Auckland, N.Z.: University of Auckland Press, 1988.

Pugsley, Christopher *On the Fringe of Hell: New Zealanders and Military Discipline in the First World War.* Auckland, N.Z.: Hodder & Stoughton, 1991.